Alex Potter

P9-CQK-250

power friending

power friending

Demystifying Social Media
to Grow Your Business

AMBER MAC

Portfolio

PORTFOLIO

Published by the Penguin Group

Penguin Group (USA) Inc., 375 Hudson Street, New York, New York 10014, U.S.A. ■ Penguin Group (Canada), 90 Eglinton Avenue East, Suite 700, Toronto, Ontario, Canada M4P 2Y3 (a division of Pearson Penguin Canada Inc.) ■ Penguin Books Ltd, 80 Strand, London WC2R 0RL, England ■ Penguin Ireland, 25 St. Stephen's Green, Dublin 2, Ireland (a division of Penguin Books Ltd) ■ Penguin Books Australia Ltd, 250 Camberwell Road, Camberwell, Victoria 3124, Australia (a division of Pearson Australia Group Pty Ltd) ■ Penguin Books India Pvt Ltd, 11 Community Centre, Panchsheel Park, New Delhi – 110 017, India ■ Penguin Group (NZ), 67 Apollo Drive, Rosedale, North Shore 0632, New Zealand (a division of Pearson New Zealand Ltd) ■ Penguin Books (South Africa) (Pty) Ltd, 24 Sturdee Avenue, Rosebank, Johannesburg 2196, South Africa

Penguin Books Ltd, Registered Offices:
80 Strand, London WC2R 0RL, England

First published in 2010 by Portfolio,
a member of Penguin Group (USA) Inc.

10   9   8   7   6   5   4   3   2   1

LIBRARY OF CONGRESS CATALOGING IN PUBLICATION DATA

Mac, Amber.
Power friending : demystifying social media to grow your business / Amber Mac.
p.   cm.
Includes bibliographical references and index.
ISBN 978-1-59184-328-3
1. Internet marketing.   2. Social media—Economic aspects.   3. Online social networks—
Economic aspects.   I. Title.
HF5415.1265.M316 2010
659.20285´6754—dc22   2009050131

Printed in the United States of America
Set in Vendetta with Agenda
Designed by Daniel Lagin

For GAR

Wish you were here

Contents

Introduction

Flying High on Social Media

I don't care if it has smooth leather seats, plush clean carpet, and fancy cup holders. When you're afraid to fly, if it's a small plane, it's a small plane. And as we (frightened) frequent fliers know, on small planes the big bumps feel even bigger. Thankfully, on this particular trip, I was sitting beside one of the world's most motivational speakers. As I gripped my sticky tan armrests thirty thousand feet over Southwestern Ontario, Tony Robbins kindly distracted me with stories of life, love, and social networking.

After I interviewed Robbins for *Webnation*, a TV show I host about how the Internet is changing the way we live, work, and play, he invited me to fly on his jet to talk about working on a new social networking project with him and his team, a project that included advising him about how to participate in the online world. Within seconds of meeting the man with the big strong handshake and the wide toothy grin, I said yes.

As I've been monitoring Web trends over the past decade there is always that point when you know that something has tipped from the hands of early adopters into the laps of the general public. I saw it happen in June 2006 when NBC started playing nice with YouTube, quickly shifting gears from demanding that the video-sharing site remove clips of its shows, such as *Saturday Night Live* skits, to leveraging the online platform as an important marketing vehicle. Another significant milestone took place in April 2009 when Oprah Winfrey posted her first message on Twitter:

> @oprah HI TWITTERS. THANK YOU FOR A WARM WELCOME. FEELING REALLY 21st CENTURY.

The entertainment mogul also started a video blog where she casually speaks to viewers from her studio office in downtown Chicago. Like any good social media marketer, she cross-promotes these clips on Twitter. It's official. The Queen of Talk will not lose her throne to the Internet, something that has become quite apparent as you watch her many digital marketing initiatives, which are bound to continue as she ends her popular daytime show and launches her own television network.

During my flight with Robbins on October 21, 2007, I also

felt the high-tech winds of change. For the first time ever, online community building wasn't just for geeks anymore. Here I was sitting with a businessman who has coached the likes of Nelson Mandela, Bill Clinton, and Michael Jordan, but today he was turning to me for advice about how to navigate the online marketing waters.

Many of my business clients and thousands of my keynote attendees, when diving into the world of social media, often complain about information overload. The social media tools evolve quickly (often with funny names), the rules change rapidly, and the technology, as shiny and improved as it gets over time, often feels more and more complex.

While working with Robbins, I watched over the course of a few months as he went from asking me basic questions about how Twitter worked, or more specifically, why anyone would want it to work, to reaching more than a million followers on the popular micromessaging site. He quickly embraced social media with such passion that in the summer of 2009 he was asked to keynote Twitter's first major conference in Los Angeles. At the popular event he started his speech by announcing, "I came here for one central reason—Twitter is a community."

Within less than a year, he had realized that this new way of communicating would keep the thousands of people who see him speak at events around the world connected with him on a regular basis. Moreover, those people who hadn't had the Tony Robbins experience in person would get a chance to reach out to him and see what he has to offer (for free online).

The evolution of his new online community is directly generating more business for this preeminent marketing entrepreneur, thanks to a tight network of people whom Robbins has friended online. In one of his recent tweets, which is the term used to describe messages sent out on Twitter, he shared this quote, demonstrating the human need for building connections, something that hasn't changed for centuries:

> @tonyrobbins "Call it a clan, call it a network, call it a tribe, call it a family. Whatever you call it, whoever you are, you need one." —Jane Howard

Your customers, partners, and employees need you to provide the digital bridge to connect them to your business. They might not know it yet, and perhaps neither do you, but in just a few years if you haven't adopted social media in a significant way you risk shutting out the best and most powerful communications channel we've ever known, a channel that values authentic interactions and power friending at its core.

For the purposes of this book, I am defining social media as Web- and mobile-based sites and applications that people are using to participate, share, create, network, and bookmark online, and often to argue and debate too. This collaborative environment and ongoing activity encourage the communal building of a collective mosaic of online knowledge. The tools and methods in this book are just as applicable to non-profits, educational institutions, and associations as they are to for-profit businesses. Any group can benefit from social media.

FRIENDS WITH BENEFITS

When I was giving a keynote speech about the do's and don'ts of social media to a roomful of bankers at a posh Miami resort in the spring of 2008, a forty-something woman named Susan sitting in the back of the room expressed the same concern as Robbins about what to do with all these amazing new communications tools. More important, Susan was curious about what she, as a businesswoman, needed to know about the strange new ways that companies are building relationships online.

"Has the Internet changed the definition of a friend," she asked, "and how does this affect my business?"

Susan's question made me think of my own experiences in the Web world. I have more than seven thousand friends on Facebook, approximately forty thousand followers on Twitter, and hundreds of thousands of viewers and listeners of my TV and Web shows. What do I call these people, the great majority of whom I've never met? Well, quite plainly, they're my friends.

Sure, these friends are not in the same category as my best friend Jenna, who boosted me up and out as we snuck out of her basement window as teenagers. Nor do these friends replace my semiregular Sunday night homemade pizza date with my friend Chris. But I now think, if I really have to be specific, of friends such as Jenna and Chris as face-to-face friends. What my Internet friends give me are connections to a wide net of people living in digital pockets all over the world. And for me and many others these friends exist well beyond Facebook, the number-one friending site in the world.

Right now I'd like to cue up Bill Withers's 1972 hit song "Lean on Me," because it's these Internet friends whom I turn to on a regular basis when I need a hand, whether it's a much-needed opinion on what digital camera I should buy, help deciding where I should eat during an upcoming trip to New York, or a formal introduction to a mutual business acquaintance on Twitter. Here's one simple example of how this new way of friending has changed the way I make purchasing decisions, an example that I shared with Susan and the audience in Miami. (For me, this was my Twitter "aha" moment when I realized how dramatically social media was changing the business world, with many companies unfortunately missing opportunities to lead the way.)

Days before leaving for a business trip to Washington, D.C., I posted a simple eighty-character message on the micromessaging site Twitter asking where I should stay in the D.C. area. Within ten minutes, I had dozens of replies that ranged from rants about the Mayflower to raves about the Hilton. These suggestions came with all the links, details, and reviews I needed to book my hotel, much more effective than scrolling through a random Google search of D.C. hotels that turns up more than a million and a half pages of results on the Web. Google results, I might add, that are not listed in any order of quality to help me make the right booking decision. Incidentally, there was not one hotel chain that participated in this online conversation, a missed opportunity by them for sure.

These friends on Twitter, and half a dozen more of my favorite social media sites, are on call 24-7 to help out, thanks to a World Wide Web that never sleeps. They are guardians of all types of information (or, more precisely, they are human filters for all types of information). There is no cost to our relationship, just a mutual desire to build a connection where ten years ago a connection could not have existed. Like many friends, they're not perfect, but I can't imagine living without them. Also, there are unspoken rules to our friendship, rules that businesses often misinterpret, causing these businesses to do more damage than good to their brands online (we'll talk more about this later).

This hotel example is just one tiny story of how millions and millions of online friends are making important decisions online, decisions that affect your business. There is a lot more to this conversation, which makes up the nine chapters of this book, such as outlining the business rules of Internet friending, detailing how to build these relationships from the ground up, and describing how to maintain these relationships with a limited budget and minimal staff. But for now I will provide a quick answer to the second part of Susan's question: how is this evolving definition of friendship affecting the way companies do business?

EXTENDING VIRTUAL HANDSHAKES

Many high performing companies are realizing that this changing definition of a friend means that word-of-mouth marketing is also changing. Not only are friends regularly discussing companies, organizations, and products online, but friends are reaching out to companies to have their say about how those companies should operate. Smart companies are extending a friendly virtual handshake to take part in the conversation. Whether they're using Twitter or one of the many sites devoted to customer service like GetSatisfaction.com, these businesses recognize the value of friendship. They realize that the door is open to personal communications and ongoing relationships on a scale that has never existed before.

Starbucks recently launched an online community called MyStarbucksIdea.com, which we'll talk about in more detail later in the book, a site intended to respond to the Starbucks customer community and to review and promote ideas. After more than six months, the site has three million unique visitors, sixty thousand ideas submitted, and hundreds of thousands of comments. A quick review of the front page on any given day displays an up-to-date feed of the most recent community ideas, such as suggesting Starbucks should advertise to local customers by zip code and a request to bring back Silk brand soy milk.

While it might not be explicit on sites like MyStarbucksIdea, the company is building a friendship-like relationship with its customers. In this case, it's all about a shared love of coffee, the social tie that binds the Starbucks community on the Web. Starbucks is using social media to create and maintain a global coffee club online.

SHOE-FRIENDLY CUSTOMER SERVICE

Amazon-owned Internet shoe retailer Zappos, which generates more than $1 billion per year in sales, focuses its online efforts on building relationships and word-of-mouth marketing rather than traditional advertising methods. The CEO, Tony Hsieh, is well known for owning just one business suit. More important, he is generating buzz for sharing his company's strategies online via his blog and other sites, which he says in a recent interview with *Adweek* has helped Zappos to generate 75 percent of orders from repeat customers who appreciate the company's culture and transparency. "It's the opposite of what most businesses do," he said. "Most try to be secret with their secret strategies."

One of Zappos's approaches includes sharing its hiring and firing strategies on the Web. The company is famous for offering its employees $2,000 to quit after the first month of training. The idea is to get rid of anyone who does not believe in the Zappos Way. It is new approaches like this that have helped Hsieh to build an army of online friends who trust that the Web's number-one shoe e-tailer is looking out for them, just as a friend would. As Hsieh recently revealed in an interview with Oprah, he's not all that passionate about shoes (he only owns a few pairs), but he has always been passionate about building meaningful relationships with customers—and thanks to the Internet, he's been able to do this.

When I shared this Zappos story, and others like it, with keynote attendees, business clients, and friends, I quickly realized that navigating this new way of doing business and practicing Internet friending is not as easy as it sounds. Individuals and companies I speak with are constantly frustrated about where to start, what sites to join, and how managing these new circles of friends is manageable at all. And there is always the unanswered question of how to measure success.

DEMYSTIFYING THE WEB SPACE

It's impossible to provide all that much guidance while white-knuckling it during a short flight, or while rushing to answer questions during a fifteen-minute Q&A session following a keynote speech. I wrote this book as a thorough and easy-to-follow guide to using the many elements of social media to effectively grow the value of your brand and your business. After meeting thousands of people who are keen to participate in the social media space, it's apparent to me that most of them could use some help getting started.

Power friending is a social media approach built around authenticity. The goal is to build a network of real friends around your brand, developing relationships based on mutual respect and support. Whether you're a mom-and-pop shop or a well-known global enterprise (or just trying to get your blog noticed), this book provides practical, easy-to-implement strategies for effective power friending. Through dozens of stories about social media successes and failures, and my own personal experiences with clients, conference attendees, and fans, I will guide you through what you need to know to take advantage of this new way of doing business so you can dive headfirst into the online marketing world—without drowning. Get ready to build up your social media strategy, one new Internet friend at a time.

Chapter one

The History

There was a time when friendship meant having a face-to-face relationship. Friends spent time together, supported one another, and exchanged gifts. In many ways, friend etiquette continues to be important online, but the methods of interaction have changed.

Today, the most common exchange between Facebook friends routinely comes in the form of a virtual poke, a gesture that does not necessarily have to be reciprocated if the feeling is not mutual. Friends retweet messages from each other on Twitter, publicly passing along the witty things the people they follow say. Friends choose one another as YouTube "favorites," anxiously anticipating their friends' next new video upload. All of the above can happen between friends who have in fact never met each other face-to-face.

Dr. Michael Wesch, who teaches cultural anthropology at Kansas State University, commented in *The New York Times* late in 2007 that since the Internet allows for some distance between friends, "that distance makes it safe for people to connect through weak ties where they can have the appearance of a connection because it's safe." Makes sense. It's much easier for me to click my way over to a company brand representative online and complain to him than it is to look up his phone information somewhere and hope that he's waiting on the other end of the line to answer my angry call.

This digital safety net means that Web users often build up huge networks of hundreds or thousands of friends. These connections throw British anthropologist Robin Dunbar's 1992 theory of maintainable social relationships into a bit of a tailspin. Dunbar's number implies that 150 people is the limit to the number of people with whom one can maintain stable social relationships. As we look to the future of Internet friending, it's evident that 150 total friends is likely to be on the low end, unless it's just on one particular site.

Facebook founder Mark Zuckerberg has said at events such as SXSW in Austin, Texas, that the average number of friends each person has on his successful social networking site is 150, which is in line with Dunbar's assumed number. But today the average person belongs to approximately three separate social networks, from such varied communities as online hangouts for pets (mediated by their devoted owners), social networks for raw food lovers, and Web destinations for individuals madly in love with convicts. As for the number of people participating on these social networks, the Pew Internet & American Life Project recently reported that the percentage of adults using these sites grew from 8 percent in 2005 to 35 percent in 2008.

While many people tend to think of social media as a recent phenomenon, with new sites like Facebook, MySpace, and Twitter popping up seemingly overnight, social networking has been around for decades. As Socialtext cofounder Ross Mayfield told me, "From day one, the Internet was used as a social technology, by the very geeks who invented things we take for granted today like e-mail. For a short period during its initial commercialization we forgot that. Recently we discovered the power of the Web was social use, accessible by everyone, so people can discover their own power when they work together."

A brief history of social media can help put today's power friending in perspective.

1960s

Professor Don Bitzer works with colleagues at the University of Illinois to design **PLATO.** PLATO allows courseware authors and students to communicate via connected terminals, forming what some would argue is the first online community. Starting in the 1970s, this community uses an early form of e-mail, chat rooms, and instant messaging.

1971

Computer engineer Ray Tomlinson sends the first **e-mail,** which is a message to himself. It is sent between two computers sitting beside each other in Cambridge, Massachusetts. Although records are fuzzy, the first e-mail is thought to be something insignificant like "QWERTYUIOP."

1979

Ward Christensen develops the first **electronic bulletin board system (BBS).** BBS's are small personal computer servers attached to phone modems. One person at a time can phone in and participate in message board discussions. Users can also share files and participate in online games.

1980s

Jarkko Oikarinen creates the first **Internet relay chat (IRC).** IRC lets people participate in text chats online in "rooms" in real time. Users use this technology to have conversations, share files, and share links.

1990s

The **World Wide Web** is widely available to the public. Previously, access to the Web was limited to the government, military, educational institutions, and a few other select groups.

1992

IBM designs the first **smartphone** prototype. The device, named Simon, features a calendar, address book, pager, phone, and many other advanced mobile features. A couple of years later it is available for sale for approximately $900.

1998

Instant messaging soars to popularity. This technology, much like IRC, allows people to have real-time conversations online. However, instant messaging becomes much more mainstream than IRC thanks to many easy-to-use software applications, such as ICQ (which stands for "I seek you").

1999

Napster, a peer-to-peer (P2P) file-sharing service, shakes up the music world. With this technology users can easily share music files with one another for free, thus putting a dent in mainstream record sales. P2P services face legal battles from their inception through the present.

LiveJournal (also called LJ), which is one of the early social networks, helps to bring blogging to the masses. This service allows users to easily create blogs and connect with friends. During this time, blogs are primarily used to share personal moments.

2002

Friendster kicks off the online friending phenomenon. This social network is built as the destination for users to connect with friends on the Web. However, its popularity only lasts for a couple of years in the United States after users repeatedly complain about the site's poor user experience.

2003

The first **flash mob** takes place in New York City in June. Participants gather together around an expensive rug in a department store and are instructed, as a group, to tell salespeople they are shopping together for a "love rug." A flash mob describes a large group of people who get together in one place to take part in some type of performance or demonstration. Flash mobs are often organized using social media tools, especially mobile technologies.

LinkedIn launches as a social network for professional relationships. The site now has more than 50 million users, many of whom use the service to find potential employers.

MySpace hits the Web with a slogan, "A Place for Friends." When each new user signs on, MySpace president Thomas "Tom" Anderson is listed as his or her first friend.

2004

Web 2.0 is born. Publisher Tim O'Reilly is associated with its creation thanks to a conference he organizes with the same name. This term begins to loosely define a new set of Web sites launching online that act much more like software applications than the static Web sites of the late 1990s.

Flickr hits the Web as a picture-sharing community for amateur photographers. The site is now owned by Yahoo! Inc. and hosts billions of photos from a worldwide database of members.

Facebook starts its world domination. Five years later, the number-one friending site in the world has 350 million users (as of December 2009).

2005

YouTube launches, allowing users to easily upload and share videos. Within months, the site's popularity explodes with amateur video content alongside professional content. In November 2006, Google acquires YouTube for a whopping $1.65B.

2005

Apple includes a **podcast** directory in its July iTunes release, which immediately propels the term *podcasting* into the mainstream. During these early days of podcasting, tech shows dominate the top podcast list.

2006

Twitter arrives online. It is often referred to as a micromessaging site, mobile social network service, or microblogging site. Users send and read messages on the site. These messages are called tweets. The Twitter service builds an army of users who love communicating in 140 characters or less.

2009

Foursquare is created. This is a location-based service that allows users to check in at certain locations to notify friends and participate in its many gaming components.

The *New Oxford Dictionary* declares **unfriend** its word of the year. It describes the new verb as "To remove someone as a 'friend' on a social networking site such as Facebook." Other new words that are considered include *hashtag*, *netbook*, and *sexting*.

FRIENDING IN THE FUTURE

The need for building elaborate social connections hasn't really changed (but the tools have). Many companies, such as AT&T, are choosing to designate a public person to represent their company online. However, online marketing for many organizations is not all that intuitive, so in the next chapters we'll discuss step-by-step what it takes to put your social media strategy into play with friending at the forefront of your online marketing plan. However, before we tackle some of the tools and strategies, let's talk fear and loathing in social media.

Chapter two

The Fears

There is a button for sale on the online shopping site Zazzle .com that reads: MY CRIB HAS WI-FI. For $6.99, parents can pick up a pin to convey the idea that their baby's nursery is Internet-enabled around the clock. While this is obviously tongue-in-cheek, the reality is that a younger generation will grow up in a world where Web connectivity is ubiquitous. Moreover, social media will become just another set of tools that are used for communication.

Don Tapscott's kids think it's pretty ridiculous that, in the early 1990s, their dad (a new media author and speaker) was invited to talk on TV about how to surf the Web. Both his son and daughter commented that watching their father on this show would have been pretty darn boring. After all, his children grew up digital, and they didn't care to obsess about how the Internet delivers content. It's what's *happening* on the Internet that interests them.

The fact that you picked up this book shows that you are interested in learning more about how to kick-start a successful social media campaign, but chances are that you or someone at your company is afraid that promoting these online tools could very easily have a negative impact on your brand. As with any new technology, it's this fear that inhibits learning more.

While I was interviewing Tapscott for a podcast I do called *net@night* on Leo Laporte's TWiT network, he commented that in the early 1980s many people he worked with did not believe that computers would ever become mainstream because that would require business executives to learn the one skill they considered reserved for clerical people: typing.

However, being slow to accept innovation into our lives is nothing new. After all, the term "Luddite," which describes a social movement in Britain where textile artists fought against new-and-improved looms, dates back to the early 1800s. For every early adopter or neophiliac addicted to new and shiny things, there are many more people resistant to new ways of doing things.

THE BRIDGE TO THE MAINLAND

Whenever I think of embracing the next big thing, I think of my grandmother. It's not that she was for innovation. In fact, she felt the opposite. She was born in Canada's smallest province, Prince Edward Island (PEI), in 1917. At the time, traveling by boat was the only way to get to and from the Island. With nine brothers and sisters and a father who died in World War I before she was even born, her family never had the money to do much traveling. Fast forward to 1997, and PEI was home to an engineering milestone. The narrowest part of the waterway separating the Island from the mainland was now joined together with the Confederation Bridge (aka the Fixed Link). This gorgeous structure is nine miles long, forming the longest bridge in the world over ice-covered waters. But my grandmother didn't think much of this new addition to her Island.

For years while it was being built she complained that it was the worst thing to happen to what was once a "sacred place." The first time we all drove across the bridge my father pulled over halfway across it so we could get out and take a closer look, despite road signs forbidding this behavior. My grandmother stayed in the backseat, vocalizing her displeasure the whole time. Now this would not be the last time Alfreda Gardiner Ricketts went on the Fixed Link. She traveled across it on dozens of family trips. Despite her fear of how this structure would bring crime to the Island, she willingly used the Confederation Bridge on a regular basis and learned to appreciate how it made all our lives easier.

While telephones, televisions, radios, and computers probably generated fear among some groups of people, my grandmother included, most of us would agree that these technologies have their advantages. If my grandmother had decided she would never cross that bridge, she would have missed out on many memorable experiences. However, if she were alive today, I'd have to do some serious convincing to get her to join Facebook, even though the number of users over age fifty-five on the social networking site grew from under one million to nearly six million during a recent six-month period.

While I just referred to social media as a communications tool like the telephone, it's easier to dial a phone than it is to manage your Twitter account. After all, to reach out and touch someone you simply need to know a few digits and make the call. With the telephone you're practicing one-on-one communication. It's great for private conversations, but if you're a company that wants to get regular messages out about your brand you're going to be leaving a lot of messages that will probably never get returned—social media requires a little more business investment up front, but there is a lot more reward on the back end. Some things are not as scary as they appear. Think of social media simply as another communications platform, despite what might be common excuses inside your organization for running in the opposite direction. After speaking to thousands of people across North America at various conferences, here are the top five reasons I've heard for not embracing social media and why none of them should stop you.

1. It's Blocked at My Office

Let me just get this one out of the way. Whether it's an office within the government, inside the education system, or within the corporate environment, there are still many environments where blocking social sites such as Facebook and YouTube is standard practice. In fact, a survey by Robert Half Technology reported late in 2009 that more than half of employers block social media Web sites. According to a survey of 1,400 chief information officers (CIOs) of companies with more than 100 employees, only 10 percent allowed employees to use social media without restrictions. While I can't physically help everyone to petition for more openness within the working environment, I can give you some ideas to help your organization change this protocol.

Many employees waste time at work. Yup, it's a fact. They might do it while hanging out in the cafeteria, talking on the phone, or taking an extra long smoke break. If employers start to clamp down on all of these things in a way that would make it impossible for employees to do them, such as cutting in-cubicle telephone lines or locking the doors to the outside after 9 A.M., many employees would quit immediately. If your organization wants to restrict access to social media Web sites, I guarantee you that this practice will, over time, push many workers to seek employment elsewhere; if you're trying to recruit a younger generation, this protocol could quite possibly could stop them from applying in the first place.

In June 2006, ITBusinessEdge.com reported results from a Telindus survey that found that 39 percent of eighteen-to-twenty-four-year-olds would consider leaving a job if Facebook was blocked. An additional 21 percent of young adults surveyed said they'd be annoyed if such a ban were put in place. Whether you like it or not, this is a trend that will continue to grow.

One reason I think employers are so uncomfortable with social media in the workplace is the public conversations it allows their employees to engage in. In their eyes, employees are not just wasting time in small groups of two or three people; they are doing so in the company of thousands online.

While it might take some time to view social media as an important part of an employee's right to communicate, if you work social media into your marketing strategy your team members can be your best allies in this world. After all, with proper social media execution, which I'll talk about later in the book, these individuals become your company's brand advocates. Their networks become your first channel to build your brand and grow your business online.

2. It's Complicated

When Canadian author Margaret Atwood was launching her new book in the fall of 2009, she invited me to her home to celebrate her latest work with her new media team. A small group of people were helping Atwood take advantage of social media to promote *The Year of the Flood*, but it was Atwood who truly embraced these tools and recognized their potential to connect to her readers online. When I walked into her home she was holding an iPhone and broadcasting her little party online (via a tool called Qik, which allows you to broadcast video live from your phone). She talked to the phone's camera from the kitchen about the different ways the audience could participate with her on the Web during her upcoming tour. She also signed copies of her book for her close friends in attendance while many of her fans tuned in on the Internet. We sat down for an informal interview following the live webcast and Atwood kindly told me about her Twitter experiences; she often refers to these new friends as her own personal cheering squad.

I bring up Atwood's social media adoption for a couple of reasons. First, she works in an industry that is thousands of years old. Also, the author is seventy years old. Instead of fearing this new technology, she is thirsty to learn more about how it works. While she doesn't believe that the electronic book is going to replace the physical book, she clearly sees many ways that new media can complement what she does. Second, she doesn't think that face-to-face promotional book events will go away either, but she realizes that she cannot be in a hundred places at one time; social media allows all of her readers to participate in conversations with her.

A quick Google search of "Margaret Atwood + social media" digs up hundreds of links, including articles in some of the world's top newspapers, mentioning how the award-winning author is leveraging online tools to market *The Year of the Flood*. Think about the press she is getting for her new book, just because she has chosen to power friend online.

Now Atwood is not a fan of complicated technology, which

is why she likes Twitter (once you get the hang of it, 140 characters is not a lot to write). When she asked me to explain to her how TweetDeck—a free software download that helps you manage your Twitter account—works, she made me promise her that learning to use the tool would be worth the time investment it required. I assured her it was. Aside from making Twitter easier to manage, aggregators like TweetDeck also allow you to manage your Facebook and MySpace accounts at the same time, making juggling multiple social networking feeds much less complicated.

3. It's Time-Consuming

Yes, it can be. It also took many of us a while to learn how to type. Remember learning the home-row on your keyboard? It wasn't easy the first time, was it? Unfortunately, we all have to start at the beginning. Today, as many of us type dozens of e-mails a day and surf hundreds of pages online, we no longer think too much about the actual keys on the keyboard. The only way most of us learned how to type well was to practice, practice, practice. None of it came fast at first, but we knew it was a skill that we would probably need in the future.

I know from dozens of keynotes that many business leaders think social media equals a big fat waste of time. But as Shel Israel argues in his book *Twitterville*, these tools simply represent a new way to connect. He writes, "I've been asked why any employer in her right mind would allow workers to tweet on company time. The answer is simple, and again it's like using the telephone at work or, for that matter, email or a fax: you use Twitter to communicate. The topic is up to you."

Depending on what day you visit the Web site Twitter, the top conversation topics can range widely, from celebrity gossip to world hunger to holiday trends. Every conversation on the site equals an opportunity for you to reach people in your target audience and join a dialogue that is meaningful to them. Instead of face-to-face conversations with these people about your brand, social media platforms like Twitter allow for these interactions to happen online. Although it might take some effort, it certainly doesn't sound like a waste of time.

The antidote to the potential time-suck of social networking is to find better ways to manage the precious time we do have. In later chapters, I'll talk about how to find the time to manage your social media efforts. Whether you have fifteen minutes or eight hours a day to build up a friend-filled community online, it is possible to build a successful strategy custom-tailored just for you.

4. It's Just for Kids

By the summer of 2009, over one-third of U.S. Facebook users were over the age of thirty-five, and about half that group was over forty-five. Early in 2009, InsideFacebook.com reported that the fastest growing demographic on Facebook was women over fifty-five. This makes me think of my mom (who is in her mid-sixties, but don't tell her I told you that). When she first started using Facebook, she stuck to playing Scrabble with my uncle. Aside from a random game here and there, she didn't see much use for the social media Web site. However, within the past couple of years she started to get friend invites from relatives and colleagues. As her network quickly grew, she realized what a wonderful resource Facebook was for keeping in touch with the people in her life. She also slowly adopted Twitter for business. She ran a local food market, so sharing deals on the micromessaging site was perfect for marketing to a small-town crowd. While social media has definitely become a preferred way for a younger generation to communicate, this is definitely not the only demographic using these tools.

5. It's Ruining Our Reputation

Since 2006, Jennifer Cisney has been Eastman Kodak's chief blogger and social media manager. Prior to taking on this role, she worked as an information designer at Kodak for more than ten years. Cisney is now the face of Kodak on a number of social media platforms including Flickr, Delicious, Facebook, and YouTube. You'll find her online giving advice about everything from how to take good pictures to where to get Kodak camera deals to how to fix your camera. Here's what Cisney told me about how her company practices authenticity online:

At Kodak we have made an effort to have our messaging come from the people who work here. Our blog posts are written by Kodak employees and we try to put our photos on our Twitter feeds. Many people have commented how nice it is to put a face with my Twitter handle @KodakCB. We think our employees are our best spokespeople . . . they love to talk about our products and hear what customers think of our products. Transparency and listening in social media is key.

Cisney runs a Kodak blog called "A Thousand Words." On the site she promotes contests in a fun and entertaining way (such as a recent "best friends" contest for the ultimate animal photos). She also came up with an idea for her blog that went viral on the Web. She attached a Kodak camera to her dog Oscar's collar with a new accessory called the Gorillapod, which is essentially a bendable tripod, put the cam on auto-timer, and posted the resulting photos to "A Thousand Words."

Among the pics was a photo of Cisney staring back at her dog, not a viewpoint pet owners get to see all that often. This little experiment encouraged other pet-owner Web users to follow suit, establishing Cisney as an authentic and respected voice inside Kodak. Not only is she monitoring the company's reputation as its eyes and ears on the Internet, she is also a driving force behind the company's reputation-building efforts on the Web. Cisney has been a speaker at social media conferences such as BlogWorld, BlogHer, and Marketing to Women. She was also named one of *Advertising Age*'s 2009 Women to Watch. Cisney's social networking approach is fundamentally proactive. In her words, "People don't necessarily want to pick up the phone and ask questions anymore. Instead they'll seek us out from wherever they are . . . Today, you can't expect everyone to come where you are. We have to go to them." If someone has something negative to say about Kodak, you can be sure that Cisney is there to win back that person's loyalty and trust.

If you don't have your own equivalent of Cisney in the social media space leading your company's active participation in the online conversation, social media has the potential to hurt your reputation online and offline. Mashable.com reported in January 2009 that social networks are now used by 26 percent of Internet users, up from 13 percent in 2006. Few predict that this percentage will decrease.

—

I regularly hear many other excuses for why companies shouldn't embrace social media, along with the disbelief that social media is here to stay. But social media is not a fad. In fact, here are just a few popular milestones and stats commonly shared online:

- Data guru Bill Tancer concludes that social media activities have surpassed porn online.
- 95 percent of businesses say they plan to use social media.
- 80 percent of companies are using or planning to use LinkedIn to find employees.

- If Facebook were a country in terms of population it would be the world's fourth largest, between the United States and Indonesia.
- As of 2009, 78 percent of social media users interact with companies or brands via new media sites and tools, an increase of 32 percent from 2008.

Whatever fears you or your organization might have about entering the social media world, opting out is simply no longer an option. But before you take the plunge and get your social media strategy under way, you need to understand and respect three critical rules.

Chapter three

The Rules

PUTTING OUT PIZZA FLAMES

On April 15, 2009, Patrick Doyle was having a bad day. The Domino's USA president had a lot more than just on-time pizza delivery on his mind. Instead, he had to find a way to quickly extinguish some online PR flames.

Two Domino's employees in Conover, North Carolina, videotaped themselves putting cheese up their nostrils and passing gas on salami before placing the toppings back on a customer's pizza, among other disgusting acts. As the incriminating clips were quickly rising up the YouTube ranks, thanks to the Twitter effect (users retweet other users' links, which often leads to links spreading rapidly), the restaurant executive was experiencing one of his worst nightmares.

Comments like this one on Consumerist.com spread across the Web:

There is a Dominos behind my apartment, I haven't ordered from them for a long time, and now I am afraid to ever order from them again.

YouTube feedback was even worse, with pages of comments like this:

This is one of the many reasons why fast-food (I consider pizza places fast-food) is BAD!

However, while the flame wars heated up, inside the corporate offices of Domino's they were tossing around ideas to try to cool things down.

Doyle, unlike many company leaders, agreed to address the controversy head-on at its source. He made a public apology in a YouTube video just a couple of days after the rapid online dissemination of his employees' nasty video. Within the first thirty seconds of his video, titled "Disgusting Domino's Pizza—Domino's Responds," Doyle thanks members of the online community for notifying his company about the foul play. Throughout the duration of the two-minute clip, Doyle continues to express how the company is taking this incredibly seriously, including felony warrants out for the employees' arrest. He then says that there is nothing more important to Domino's than its customers' trust.

It is not possible to watch Doyle's video without feeling the executive's sincerity. In fact, with hundreds of thousands of views, the Domino's president's video helped to smooth things over for his customers online. Months later, Doyle's YouTube video is home to comments like this one, showing support for the company:

> Dominos is probably the safest place to eat right now because managers are probably watching their employees like hawks, and employees aren't going to pull crap like this 'cause they don't want to get in trouble.

Doyle and his team took advantage of the same tools that the former (yes, they were quickly fired) employees used to earn back their customers' attention and trust. Instead of hiding under a rock, Domino's listened well to the chatter online, and responded better. Moreover, Doyle's team followed the rules of the social media playground. I call these rules the ABCs of Inter-

net friending, and every business must know them before ⟨
ing the online space.

A IS FOR AUTHENTICITY

The first rule about authenticity is that you don't talk about authenticity. Well, at least not publicly. The people who achieve success on the Web, whether it's a twenty-year-old student who started a multimillion-follower fashion blog on Tumblr or an eighty-year-old grandmother who launched the number-one video blog on YouTube, represent real passion to their audiences. They don't harp on about authenticity, but they do present themselves in an authentic way. Perhaps the best example of an authentic voice in the land of the Web is a wine lover from New Jersey with a funny last name.

The Wine Guy

Gary Vaynerchuk, or @garyvee as he's known on Twitter, is authentic to the core. While running a wine retail business in Springfield, New Jersey, in 2006 the entrepreneur decided to launch an online video show called *Wine Library TV*. Each weekday, he sits down in front of a camera and reviews wine. Seems simple enough, but what makes Gary such a huge hit is his passion for all things vino. In April 2009, the charismatic host shot an episode of his famous show while on a plane en route to Las Vegas. With more than four hundred comments on this one sin-

gle episode, including feedback about Gary's choice of airline—
"That is so awesome that you fly Southwest like a real person and
not some other airline in First Class only! GaryVee—KEEPIN'
IT REAL!!!"—Gary is definitely an unpretentious voice in the
wine world. For many, this is refreshing. Perhaps young blogger
Brody Clemmer describes Gary best in a post titled "I Want
to Be Gary Vee": "He has made his fortune and claimed his
fame by being himself, something that many of the companies
and people forget how to do."

The Web celebrity's success with his fan base, including
approximately a million followers on Twitter, has led him to
appearances on the talk show circuit, a multivolume book
deal, and a wine cruise that he hosts for his fans. He calls this
trip the Thunder Cruise, where he and a couple hundred wine
enthusiasts spend a week on a ship together traveling throughout the Caribbean. The Thunder Cruisers were all in attendance
to learn more about wine from Vaynerchuk, but also to get close
to the guy on the Web who they've turned into a celebrity.

There are not too many brands in the world that could convince their customers to spend their own money floating around
the sea for a week with them. With Gary, his fans couldn't
wait to jump on board. Sure, these fans love wine, but for the
most part what they love even more is the connections they've
built with Gary and his community.

Too many companies put up corporate walls that don't allow
their audiences to get close to them. When their audiences do get
close, they often feel as though they're getting the runaround.

From the automated responses from our telephone companies to the sales clerk who is too lazy to go check for more sizes, we are so used to not truly encountering an authentic experience that many of us just don't expect it anymore or anywhere.

Tattoo-Gate Down Under

In January 2009, Queensland, Australia, kicked off an online contest dubbed "The World's Best Job." The tourism bureau offered the winner a six-month job as a blogger, including a $100,000 salary, to look after a Great Barrier Reef island. Each applicant had to submit a one-minute online video detailing why he or she should get the gig. Within days the contest site came to a crashing halt with hundreds of thousands of visitors looking for more information. When the site came back to life online, the most popular video résumé featured a young woman getting a tattoo of the Great Barrier Reef to prove her commitment as a contestant.

I remember watching this video. Like many people, I couldn't believe that someone would go as far as getting a tattoo to win a contest. What was even more interesting was that she video-taped the entire tattooing process for everyone to see, so clearly this woman would be in the running for "The World's Best Job." After all, it was written in permanent ink on her body.

However, within two weeks of the contest launching, the unthinkable happened. Word came out online that she was an employee of the ad agency that managed the Queensland campaign, and her tattoo was a fake. This is a big no-no in the Web world. Trying to fake authenticity is possibly even worse than never possessing it at all. "The World's Best Job" contest was gaining international attention, getting press worth millions of dollars (much more than they initially put into the campaign). In an instant, they risked losing their credibility.

Fortunately for them, they did act quickly. On the same day the news of the fake video started to spread, Tourism Queensland's head honcho went online to admit the organization's mistake. Anthony Hayes told ABC News:

Obviously we've messed up so there's no point saying anything other than that. I've got to cop that on the chin. That's our fault and we've now cleaned it up by getting rid of it as quickly as we could. . . . It was really just to get people thinking how creative could their own video be. . . . People are off and running so we've got rid of it to make sure there's no more confusion.

The negative press did not go that much further than this, thanks to the high-level executive (quickly!) admitting they had messed up. As a result, the applications continued to pour in and the online buzz returned to daydreaming about "The World's Best Job." Yes, despite the lack of authenticity at the beginning of the campaign, an authentic response, in the end, saved the tourism bureau.

If you can start to build your strategy with authenticity top-of-mind, Internet friending will get a whole lot easier. But authenticity alone isn't enough. Along with authenticity, you need to have some brave ideas and consistent behavior.

B IS FOR BRAVERY

Social media is leading us into a brave new world, a world where everyone wants to get personal with you or your company. To survive these times, bravery is one of the keys to success. Being brave means dealing with criticism (which we'll discuss in more detail in chapter 5), but it also means coming up with innovative ideas. With so much noise online, your social media presence has to be special to stand out.

Pepsi Turfs the Super Bowl

In December 2009, Pepsi announced that it would not advertise during the Super Bowl. Instead, the company launched a $20-million social media campaign that will fund thousands of community projects (based on community feedback). As ESPN .com reported, this move marks the end of Pepsi's twenty-three-year ad run during one of the biggest annual sporting events in the United States (in 2009, PepsiCo Inc. spent approximately $33 million during the Super Bowl). After years of relying on high-powered celebrities such as Britney Spears, Cindy Crawford, and Ozzy Osborne, the company is now putting its marketing power into the hands of everyday people. With its new

Refresh Project, Pepsi is asking the public to vote on a cause they care the most about. The campaign's question to the masses: Can a soda make the world a better place? Pepsi is putting on a brave face as they head into unchartered waters and leave the Super Bowl television ad opportunity behind.

Trading Burgers for Friends

In January 2009 Burger King's latest Web campaign claimed that while "Friendship is strong, the Whopper is stronger." The fast-food joint launched a Facebook application called Whopper Sacrifice that challenged the idea that online friends were really that important.

When you downloaded the tiny piece of software within Facebook, you had the option to dump ten friends in exchange for a coupon for a free Whopper (the names of the friends you dumped were listed publicly in your news feed and their animated profile pics burned up on your screen). The campaign's tagline? "Who will be the next to go?" Within days of going online, news about the app hit every major tech news blog and mainstream media. The very question of whether unfriending was acceptable, or not, inspired heated conversations online.

Twitter user @krystyl wrote: "The Facebook Whopper sacrifice has gotten out of control . . . I am getting random friend requests so they can burn me as a sacrifice." Another Twitter user, @JustinRZB, replied that "I will GLADLY sacrifice friends for a tasty whopper." With hundreds of thousands of Facebook applications on the Web, Burger King knew that they had to find a way to break through the clutter. And that is just what they did, but not without consequences.

Within one week of the campaign going live, more than 190,000 friends had been sacrificed. The campaign was a success in terms of getting people to discuss Burger King. The agency behind the initiative told Adweek.com that "The [friend] removal is another kind of socializing. At first you think it's anti-social, but it's a social device. Now we finally have something to talk about." However, within two weeks, and after almost a quarter of a million friends were unfriended on Facebook, Burger King pulled the promo. Turns out that a Facebook spokesperson said the notice sent to unfriended friends was an invasion of privacy on a site that doesn't notify users if their friends drop them. Moreover, while this campaign made a brave statement and got people talking, many users found the company's antics offensive (after all, no one wants to be a victim of unfriending). Even on Facebook, some potential customers will be offended by intrusive corporate campaigns reaching their long fingers into their social relationships.

The Motrin Moms Headache

Throughout this book I'll talk more about what strategies make the most sense for your organization. When you figure out how to work these strategies into your plan, it's critical to follow this second rule or else you could face thousands of mommy bloggers destroying your brand over one short weekend.

In November 2008, Motrin launched an online video campaign just before the weekend. The video was intended as a "We feel your pain" type of ad, but instead of commiserating with mothers, they wound up doing quite the opposite. The ad unintentionally insinuated that mothers who were carrying their babies around in slings and other devices were only doing so to be fashionable. The ad then suggested that these moms take Motrin to relieve the stress of looking "tired and crazy." After only a few short hours the video went viral online and the ad became one of the most popular topics on Twitter. By Saturday night, hundreds of moms on Twitter were outraged about the video, which also implied that carrying your baby around is only a good idea "in theory." By Sunday afternoon, hundreds of moms were blogging and bashing Motrin. Mom Barb Lattin wrote this on her site:

> Ibuprofin [*sic*] is what works best for me, and Motrin has always been my favorite brand of ibuprofin. I'm reconsidering this. Why? Because their new campaign bashes babywearing.

It took until Monday afternoon for Motrin to officially respond to the negative feedback. Finally, they removed the video and posted a formal apology from their head of marketing, a mother of three, on their Web site. After a few weeks the ad was discontinued in print form, too. Unfortunately for Motrin, the damage was done. Many moms and critics online wrote that the pharmaceutical company should have responded much earlier, so that the Motrin Web hate-on had a shorter lifespan. The Motrin Moms Headache is now known in blogging circles as MotrinGate.

We'll talk more about listening and responding to new friends within this chapter, but the lesson here is that when you launch any type of campaign on the Web you need to be an active voice in the community as soon as that campaign goes live. If you don't do this, and if there is any criticism, your brand can easily turn into an online punching bag. In short, be brave *and* ready to respond.

C IS FOR CONSISTENCY

Imagine going to your local grocery store and one day they're out of milk. The next week, they're out of coffee. Finally, in the third week, they're out of bread. By the end of the month, you're going to stop going back. In the social media world, just like the grocery world, consistency is key. When your audience finds out that you are participating on a site, they expect you to be there.

Often businesses get on the right track by beginning to engage online, but they fail to commit on a long-term basis. For a few weeks they blog regularly or update their Twitter account, but as time goes on they eventually lose interest in social media and abandon their accounts. Let's face it, we've all seen it happen. Just the other day I was checking out a retailer's blog and they hadn't written a new post in almost six months. Six months! With a lack of consistency like this, it's impossible to truly convince your audience that you care about having a conversation with them.

The Yellowknife Yamaha Example

One mistake marketers often make when they enter the social media space is that as soon as they start participating in online communities, they expect friends to come to them. This rarely happens. To make friends, it's important to play in the circles where people are already talking about your brand. For example, Yamaha's senior product and research manager Chris Reid runs a company blog called "Sled Talk," with a stated mandate to connect with the company's sledding community on a personal level: "keep it deep and real, don't ask me to look up the ring end gap for your Inviter or beat on me because you baked your hy-fax on Kevlar Lake and I'll try to keep the lid on the corporate whitewash bucket." While managing his blog, Reid frequently visits online sledding communities to find out what customers are saying about his Yamaha products. During one of his routine visits to a Web forum he noticed that an active customer, who called himself Yellowknife, was extremely critical of a specific Yamaha trailer part. Instead of arguing with Yellowknife, Reid decided to openly (and officially) request the customer's input to design a better product for Yamaha, which turned into a great PR story for the company since a new design was now based on direct customer feedback. If Reid did not visit communities consistently, he would have missed making this connection. Without consistency, you risk upsetting your audience.

Southwest Lands a JetBlue Customer

Shashank Nigam is a well-known airline marketer and blogger. While attending South by Southwest, the popular new media and music convention in Austin, Texas, he was trying to reach out to JetBlue on Twitter to inquire about his delayed flight back to San Francisco. JetBlue sent one message to Nigam, but then appeared to ignore his subsequent requests. Since Nigam was getting nowhere with his attempts to try to contact JetBlue, he decided to take his flight fate into his own hands. He put out a request to Southwest Airlines on Twitter to see if they could get him to San Francisco faster. Southwest returned his messages promptly and continued to present Nigam with some options for his return. Nigam in turn blogged about this experience:

> If you are a company, you see an unhappy customer out there, you need to move quick and communicate! @JetBlue

could have said "got your tweet, will follow up soon" something to let me know they were working on it. Something... just let me know you have not forgot about me.

Although JetBlue is an active player on the social media scene, in this specific instance consistency was key. Once you start to engage, as JetBlue did with Nigam, you need to follow through on the conversation.

SOPHIE THE TWEET-HAPPY GIRAFFE NAILS THE ABCS

One of the comments I hear from my business clients and keynote attendees is that they want to be consistent, but they often don't know what to say in the social media world. They often feel that they lack the creativity to truly participate in an engaging way. However, with some creative brainstorming with your team, you might be surprised to learn new ways to connect online. To show you what I mean, I want to introduce you to a giraffe named Sophie.

Since 1961, this brown-spotted plastic animal has landed in the hands (well, more specifically, mouths) of millions and millions of babies. Handmade in France, Sophie is a natural rubber nontoxic squeaky teether and toy. At around $20 each, she's not cheap. However, she is loved offline and online.

Yes, Sophie is on Twitter. If you're ever wondering how your business could have a lot to say, just take a peek at Sophie's tweets. On average she sends out a few messages a day, mostly replying to new parents who recently bought the toy. What makes this Twitter account unique is not necessarily that it's a plastic giraffe tweeting, but the effort that the account owner has put into regularly finding news about all things Sophie. Every week, Sophie sends out links to photos of babies carrying Sophie, messages from moms talking about Sophie in online forums, and press reviews of Sophie. There is never a day that goes by without some kind of Sophie news. This is a great example of all three ABCs of Internet friending in action.

Sophie's tweets are authentic—rather than shilling for the product, the people running the account make a special effort to create tweets that are meaningful to Sophie's followers. It's a brave campaign—who knew a tweeting plastic giraffe would be such a hit? And Sophie is consistent: she regularly updates her account and responds to her many fans.

THE VIRAL TACO TRUCK

A small business in Los Angeles has also learned how to make social media work for them as they spin around the city cooking up delicious treats. The Kogi Korean BBQ-To-Go taco trucks zip around town catering to thousands of diehard fans. Like Sophie, these owners have created a compelling online presence. With more than forty thousand followers on Twitter, the small business owners consistently post where they'll be serving tacos every day (always accepting suggestions from fans). They also mention if they're running late or if one of their trucks has broken down. On their Web site they run a blog, which is updated on a regular basis with behind-the-scenes stories. Their Flickr account, which is featured prominently on their Web site, includes photos of the company owners and employees, and day-in-the-life moments. Thanks to such successful social media usage, the trucks are often greeted with hundreds of hungry fans who will wait more than an hour for the famous food. Those who are following the viral taco truck are often considered to be part of what's now called "Kogi Kulture."

From a restaurant executive getting his company out of hot water to a socially engaged rubber giraffe and a creative taco truck promotion, there is a place for every business in the social media world. The key thing is to understand the tools available to you and how to use them effectively, which I'll cover in the next few chapters.

Chapter four

The Tools

CARPENTRY AT ITS BEST

My friend Jenna, whom I briefly mentioned at the beginning of the book, is an orthopedic sales rep. When she first started her job, she spent hours on end studying the elaborate contents of various metal trays, complete with dozens of instruments that surgeons need to replace knees, hips, shoulders, and elbows. She likes to describe orthopedic surgery as "carpentry at its best," since some of the instruments required include saws, drill bits, and other parts. Knowing how each of these instruments work is critical to ensure that each procedure is performed in a timely and efficient manner. More important, using these tools properly is key to ensuring the safety of the patient waiting on the operating table.

Although the state of affairs during joint replacement surgery is much more serious than the state of your marketing plan, for some businesses using the wrong social media tools can often mean the death of your brand. After all, word of mouth is the next killer marketing app. If the Web world turns on you, chances are that you could have a rough ride into the future. I'll talk more about social media failures in chapter 7, including how some companies ignored the ABCs of power friending, but for now let's focus on the social media instruments that will provide a solid foundation for your organization in this space. There are seven broad categories of tools, along with a few great gadgets, to get your strategy under way. And the good news is that there are no saws or drill bits or heavy lifting required, unless you're in the blender-making business in Utah.

YOUR TOOLS CHECKLIST

- ➡ **Blogs**—A blog is an online journal that is most often a public destination for your company to share its news, events, and other interesting content.
- ➡ **Micromessaging**—A micromessaging site, such as Twitter, allows users to communicate in short-form messages (as compared to long-form blogs).
- ➡ **Social Networking**—A social network is an online service that serves to connect audiences. The most popular social networks are Facebook and LinkedIn, although there are thousands of niche-oriented social networks with dedicated communities online.

➤ **Videos**—Video should be a component of most social media campaigns. Whether you're creating a corporate introduction for your Web site, a how-to demo or a mobile ad, video is one of the best ways to communicate your brand.

➤ **Podcasts**—A podcast is an online video or audio show that is most often accessed via a feed or subscription service. Podcasts are quite often educational, so viewers or listeners can learn something for free.

➤ **Mobile Tools**—A mobile tool in the social media space is most often an application that is downloaded on a smartphone, such as an iPhone, BlackBerry, Android, or other device. There are free and paid apps, and with more than a billion online they serve a wide variety of functions.

➤ **Wikis**—A wiki is an online collaborative tool that anyone can edit (when given the proper permissions). Wikipedia is the most well-known wiki, but wikis are also popular inside and outside organizations to build central repositories of information.

BLOGS

Blogs, originally called weblogs, provide an online home for anyone to write publicly available journal-like entries. When blogs first launched online, via services such as LiveJournal in the late 1990s, users most often talked about mundane topics such as what they ate for breakfast or a cool trick their cat just did. Since their creation, most blog services have also provided a comments field for each entry, or post. Today, popular online blogging tools such as WordPress (which is a popular free publishing platform) provide functionality to make a blog a great home base for all your social media efforts (for example, you can use WordPress plug-ins (which are downloads that enhance Wordpress) that can easily pull in all types of information to your blog, including video or photo feeds). The corporate world has discovered that blogs can be an effective way to convey a company's message, often replacing the traditionally stuffy press release. At some companies, blogs are now a prime destination for an organization to get information about what it does on the inside to the outside world, which also leads to community building efforts to expose positive corporate cultures and practices to the outside world. Jason Fried's company is a good example of this.

"There are no secrets anymore," Fried commented during a podcast interview with me. "You can't stop someone from doing something anymore. So we figured, you know what, at the end of the day it's just going to benefit everybody and that's a good thing." Fried is the founder of 37signals, a software developer that is also a leader in the corporate blogging world. Their "Signal vs. Noise" blog has approximately 100,000 subscribers. 37signals rarely blogs about their products, but instead shares advice about business, design, editorials, and other topics in the Web space. Their blog became so popular as a beacon in the Web development industry that 37signals decided to write a practical business book called *Getting Real*. Instead of printing copies of the book, 37signals sold PDF copies for $19 a download. They quickly sold more than $350,000 worth of the popular e-books, mostly to friends of the company who believed in the 37signals philosophy for building Web applications. While not all blogs can easily generate revenue, if you create good content the community will come.

Industry Expert

Real estate site Zillow has always been a step ahead in the real estate field with its authentic voice in dealing with mortgage loans. But now the company has added another asset to its business—a successful blog that proves Zillow.com really understands that its audience is heading to the Web to get information first. According to the 2009 National Association of Realtors Profile of Home Buyers and Sellers, 87 percent of home buyers used the Internet in their search for a new place to live. As a result of this Internet search, 77 percent drove by or viewed a home that they first saw on the Web. The Zillow blog doesn't just post information about how to buy a home; Zillow has also created a content strategy that includes a wide range of topics that might interest its audience. From interesting posts on "National Good Neighbor Day" to how much your favorite celebrity's house is worth, there is a lot of personality in the writing. On the list of hot topics on the blog, you will find everything from the $8,000 tax credit for first-time home buyers to a review of Sarah Palin's Alaska home.

The posts are rarely self-promotional and lend themselves to two-way conversation. This is key because most corporate blogs are merely republications of press releases, a big no-no in the blogging world, and receive very few comments and readers. Zillow's blog, on the other hand, is a wonderful example of how expert advice goes a long way with niche audiences, such as those interested in real estate. Zillow's is one of the top four most visited real estate sites in the world and has as many as nine million unique viewers per month. It also has a widely popular iPhone application, among other technology initiatives that are displayed prominently on its blog (showing that Zillow is properly integrating various elements of its social media strategy).

Community Content

Articulate is an e-learning tools company. Their blog is one of the most read e-learning blogs in the industry with more than twenty thousand subscribers. It's known for its great content and the many conversations that take place within its comments section. The blog has its own host, Tom Kuhlmann, who puts a friendly face on the company. Here's Tom's welcome message, which is prominent on the site:

Hi, I'm Tom, your host of The Rapid E-Learning Blog. I am passionate about learning and technology. I have over 15 years experience in the training industry where I've developed hundreds of hours of elearning and managed elearning projects at Capital One, Washington Mutual, and Weyerhaeuser.

The blog has steadily spread in popularity mainly due to word of mouth from its ever-growing community of brand advocates in the e-learning space, which has undoubtedly led to the company's sales success. The blog's content focuses on "practical real-world tips for e-learning success" and helps e-learners find new and clever ways to relate to the material to achieve better results in their efforts.

MICROMESSAGING

So much has been written about Twitter and how and why, or more often why not, to use the 140-character-based messaging service. From the anchor desks of CNN soliciting viewer pictures and comments for the news of the day to the monologues of the late-night crowd, the question of the day is, To Tweet or Not to Tweet? The simple answer is yes—tweet! You can accomplish a lot with a micromessaging site like Twitter.

Of course, there are exceptions. One of my company's clients is the American Dental Association (ADA). Although they might be very interested in using Twitter, the reality is that they cannot distribute oral hygiene advice online without risking liability. Legally approved content sharing is key for the Association. For this reason, we chose to create a podcast for the ADA called *Straight from the Mouth*. These videos, which deliver carefully planned advice, are posted online on a monthly basis. The extended time frame between episodes allows the legal department to thoroughly evaluate each episode's content. However, many organizations are not so legally bound and may consider a more casual approach, including delivering customer service 140 characters at a time.

Customer Service

Comcast, the U.S. cable giant, has had a less than successful online experience. Some brand reputation surveys have placed Comcast just above famous bad boys like Halliburton and subprime mortgage lender Countrywide. Needless to say, many Comcast customers have not been satisfied with their cable service, and they often vented in online forums. A popular blog called "ComcastMustDie" used to be customers' number-one complaining destination online. More recently, Comcast started an innovative customer service campaign on a number of sites including Twitter. Their account, ComcastCares, is now where subscribers go to get customer support. One such subscriber made a complaint on Twitter about the lackluster quality of his HD picture during a Boston Celtics game, and within minutes

ComcastCares responded to the customer and sent someone out the next day to fix the signal. The subscriber then wrote on his blog, "Now my HDTV rocks! THAT my friends is customer service and how it should work all the time." This is the power of instant micromessaging. Sure, the majority of tweets you see run across Twitter's home page may seem superficial on the surface, but the immediacy and openness of the platform offers a wonderful opportunity to connect and have valuable customer conversations, complete with positive feedback and negative criticism.

Customer Feedback

Southwest Airlines now uses Twitter to engage directly with customers. Southwest monitors tweets and Facebook statuses so it can reach out to its customers with gratitude if there are positive mentions of the carrier or to lend a helping hand if a passenger is frustrated with the service. When Travis Johnson recently complained via Twitter about his check-in process with the airline, Southwest—within minutes—sent Johnson a public response stating, "So sorry to hear it! What don't you like about the check-in process? Did your flight get off okay?" Now this digital comforting may not soothe all customer complaints, but as Southwest Airlines spokesperson Christi Day told *The Boston Globe*, "We monitor those channels because we know these conversations are taking place there, and we can either watch the conversations or take part in them." A proactive approach will almost always result in an increase in customer satisfaction.

Social Causes

A well-known meat company from Arkansas is using Twitter as a platform for its hunger relief campaign efforts. Tyson Foods wanted to promote its food donation efforts throughout the country in a way that would reach out to the general public, so Ed Nicholson, the company's director of PR and community—and social media guru—chose to hit Twitter to spread the company's message. Nicholson had already been using conventional blogging techniques, but like many bloggers, he gravitated toward Twitter to continue to communicate a message. Tyson Foods' Twitter page has approximately five thousand followers and serves as a canvas for Tyson Foods to explore its efforts, but also allows and encourages other users to describe their own hunger relief efforts as well. Nicholson has done an excellent job as a connector, reaching out to other hunger relief organizations like Meals on Wheels on Twitter and posting links to hunger stats, such as the fact that five million U.S. citizens go to bed hungry on a regular basis. Tyson Foods has created a sense of community around the cause without focusing on self-promotion, which is key. However, Nicholson is not alone in the hunger fighting campaign on Twitter. One of his popular tweets includes a link to a blog post he wrote featuring more than one hundred people on Twitter who are active in the hunger discussion both online and offline. Thanks to this post, dozens of people included on the list commented on the Tyson Foods' "Hunger Relief" blog.

SOCIAL NETWORKING

Paula Drum was the VP of marketing for the financial advice company H&R Block until she went on to pursue other business ventures. In the time she spent with H&R Block she completely turned its marketing strategy around and solidified the company's position as a positive example of how to successfully utilize social media tools. Her plan was to help the company set out overarching general goals it wanted to achieve. From there, Drum helped H&R Block join many social media communities where these goals could be leveraged across the board. These diverse communities include but are not limited to Second Life, Twitter, Facebook, MySpace, YouTube—even eHarmony.com! Drum also helped the company set up its very own online community named Digits. The idea was to reinforce brand awareness and present the company as innovative by providing unexpected and meaningful interactions with users.

For example, a user could stop by a virtual H&R Block building in Second Life, an online virtual world that was a popular corporate marketing destination a couple of years ago, and have a real-time conversation with an H&R Block avatar—who would be run by a financial expert with the company.

Drum was successful in leveraging a number of social networks, including a custom branded social network. Although many of the tools described in this book can fall within the social network category, for our purposes in this chapter I'm defining a social network as a Web destination where the main purpose is to maintain a network of friends. Some of the most popular social networks for business marketing include Facebook, My-Space, and LinkedIn.

Managing Multiple Social Network Accounts

With marketing budgets shrinking in almost every industry, the added task of managing social media initiatives is getting bigger. However, there are easy ways to manage multiple social networks at the same time. For example, there are tools to update Twitter with your Facebook status and vice versa. Also, if you choose to post a lot of photos on your Twitter account, you can use a tool called Flickr2Twitter (which is simply a unique e-mail address that you register for on Flickr) to save these pictures on Flickr while sending the photo links to Twitter at the same time. This means that you have an ongoing archive of all the pictures you promote on Twitter saved automatically on Flickr. There are also tools online such as Atomkeep that will allow you to manage your social media profiles on the most popular sites in one place.

VIDEOS

What's red, black, and white, and gets a billion views a day? If you guessed YouTube, you're bang on. Three years after Google bought the video-sharing site for $1.65 billion, YouTube is getting substantially more daily eyeballs than the top television networks in the United States combined.

"We thought we had a good idea," said YouTube cofounder Steve Chen when I interviewed him in March 2006. Neither of us realized at the time that this comment from the entrepreneur was probably the biggest understatement of the Internet age. During our conversation, he told me about the early days of YouTube. He talked about how the idea for the site started casually at a dinner party with some friends in January 2005. They realized how easy it was for them to share photos, but passing video around electronically was a different story. A couple months later, he and his team started YouTube. "It's slowly hitting us that we're hitting the mainstream," Chen commented to me, just a few months after the site's official launch. At the time of our interview, YouTube was getting approximately 30 million views a day and had only twenty-two employees. "There's a lot of excitement here," said Chen. "We're still a small company. I think the best part is that we're able to move so quickly." Well, they sure did move. Jumping from 30 million views a day to one billion is a pretty substantial leap. As of early 2009, there were thirteen hours of video uploaded to YouTube every minute. The video-sharing site was also ranked as the world's second largest search engine, just behind Google.

Although there is excitement about the number of videos now available online, as we all know, the majority of these videos aren't all that good. The quality of the information on a site like

YouTube is similar to the experience of clicking through hundreds of cable channels: sometimes there is just absolutely nothing on. Worse yet, our attention span for watching online videos is far shorter than for television shows. The average length of a YouTube video is just under three minutes, which gives us a little insight into the type of video content that works on the Web. In the social media space, there are a few different types of video approaches that have a proven track record.

Authentic Corporate Culture: Will It Blend?

Blendtec, a high-end blender manufacturer from Utah, was relatively unknown in the online world before its marketing director, George Wright, identified a unique opportunity on the company's factory floor. Wright was watching Blendtec's CEO Tom Dickson blending a two-by-four (yes, a giant piece of lumber!) as a stress test for new blender parts. Wright was fascinated. He soon launched an initiative to take these routine "test run" videos to the masses online. Instead of hiring an actor to do the demos and an expensive advertising agency to shoot them, Wright spent a few hundred dollars on camera equipment and asked Dickson to do the blending on camera.

Very quickly, the videos were raking up the views online. Search "will it blend" on YouTube and find a video of Dickson with the Blendtec blender mixing up a bag of fifty marbles with more than three million views; this is just one of dozens of examples from the ongoing experiment (as the videos say, do not try this at home). Aside from significant online exposure, Dickson made appearances on late night talk shows, such as *The Tonight Show* with Jay Leno in 2007. Since the Will It Blend? campaign began, the organization has blended everything on camera from a new iPhone to a Nintendo Wii controller. Blendtec publicly credits these videos with helping to drive sales of the consumer blender up 500 percent in 2007. After all, everyone wants to be friends with a company that looks like a fun place to work.

Wright told me, "I have learned that if you produce compelling content, it is practically impossible to stop it from spreading. Blendtec has become a household name and has achieved the brand awareness that was intended. If you do not believe that social media is a valuable marketing tool, then you will simply have a hard time competing in the evolving marketplace."

The Blendtec example above is just one type of video used for building community online, one that aims to share authentic company culture. Online brand-building can also be achieved through tutorials and user-generated content.

Company "Tutorial" Commercials: Alltop Is on Top

Another kind of video that can be incredibly successful is the tutorial. Among the top players in the field is Common Craft, whose catchy cartoonish videos are terrific at teaching the basics of Web technologies like RSS, social networking, wikis, and more. This agency's videos are so successful that many companies have hired the small team to create introductory videos for them describing what their companies do. The tutorial genre even has its place on CBS News, where Josh Landis and Mitch Butler do a whiteboard animation of topics in the news. One example of a simple online tutorial that helps its viewers understand what the company is all about is Guy Kawasaki's RSS aggregator Alltop. The video is under a minute and a half long yet gives a clear and concise explanation of how to navigate and use the site. It shows you how to bypass clumsy RSS readers entirely and create your own reading lists for all your varied interests, from dolls to dollars. The clean graphics and friendly music make the video, and by extension the site, much more accessible to the user.

Alltop is an "online magazine rack" that allows anyone to easily pull together a dynamic reading list based on a variety of chosen topics. The service is based on aggregated RSS (really simple syndication) feeds. In non-geek-speak, what this means is that Alltop basically provides a filter to prevent information from becoming overwhelming. Click on Health and there are dozens of subcategories where you can dig into the latest links on specific topics, from acne to STDs. Knowing that "RSS" is kind of a scary term for a lot of nontechies, Alltop created a simple how-to video demonstrating the purpose of their Web site. The YouTube video is a great example of how a company can benefit significantly from creating a video explanation describing what a company is all about. Thanks to some catchy music, cute graphics, and easy-to-understand language, the whole video experience is as simple as the site itself.

User-Generated Content: Mortgage Movies

Instead of pushing out a typical marketing campaign, Quicken Loans, America's largest online lender, has turned to its customers to produce user-generated content to promote the business. Participants were asked to discuss their unscripted experiences and feedback with the mortgage company. Getting someone to care about a mortgage company isn't easy, so Quicken did something smart to kick-start the conversation. In a homemade video, the Rodriguezes, a family of five from New Mexico, spoke about how Quicken Loans helped them to refinance their mortgage, which allowed them to invest in property and do some home renovations. Not only did the family share their stories, they took viewers on a tour of their home. Quicken featured the Rodriguez video and more on its YouTube channel, a place where families nationwide are able to upload their videos and share them with viewers who may be considering the company's services. Real stories are often a better form of advertising than classic advertisements, and Quicken Loans proves it with its user-generated YouTube channel. Now this campaign isn't perfect, as it takes a lot of effort to produce good video content online, which we'll talk about in chapter 6, "The Execution," but it is a step in the right direction.

PODCASTS

A podcast is an audio or video show that is released online. Most often, these shows are downloaded for free using services like iTunes. When podcasts originally launched on the Web there were not many companies producing this type of content. Over the past few years, this has changed dramatically. In 2005 a top podcast on iTunes would often be an independent technology show, created by a small team in an informal environment. For example, I created my video podcast *commandN* in June 2005 with some cheap technology and at one point we hit the number-one spot on the iTunes podcast directory (thanks to our focus on weekly tech news for an online audience who was thirsty for more of this type of content).

Today, big companies (mostly media) own the top podcast lists. This doesn't mean that there isn't room in the podcast space for your organization. In fact, there is unlimited room. While big media podcasts may own the top charts, there is no better example of Chris Anderson's "long tail" than in this space. *Wired* magazine's Anderson talks about the long tail as "millions of niche markets at the shallow end." In other words, there are thousands of unique podcasts that cater to vibrant, but perhaps lesser known, communities. Unlike traditional media, podcasts are typically shorter in length and are less formal than a television or radio show since anyone can create one.

Leo Laporte, a colleague of mine and the undeniable king of podcasting, spoke at the Online News Association (ONA) conference in San Francisco in 2009 about how his podcast empire, TWiT.tv, has become successful. "We're talking directly to the audience of our friends, who are not only engaged, but they trust us." This was Laporte's key message at the ONA conference. Laporte's TWiT.tv network is a collection of more than a dozen online shows that center around technology conversations. The network launched in 2005, with just one podcast at the helm. Although I continue to use the term "podcast," as Leo mentioned at the ONA event, the techie term is on its way out.

It is often difficult for the average person to figure out how to find a podcast in iTunes or another online store, subscribe to the podcast, and then get the podcast on his or her device. For this reason, it's key to make your podcast available in a directory but also make it easy to download on your Web site. If you're serving a low-tech audience, you might also want to describe what a podcast is to them (and refer to it simply as a "show"). What makes this tool an excellent way to participate in the social media space is that you can build your own TV or radio program for a tiny fraction of what it would have cost ten years ago. Depending on your audience, skills, and budget, you can create either an audio or a video show. In some cases, it might make sense to do both.

Audio Shows

The Canadian Bar Association (CBA) started a podcast series hosted by CBA's Web producer, Mark Kuiack. The online radio show, entitled *CBA PracticeLink*, is designed with their audience in mind. Because their target demographic is busy lawyers, their episodes focus on one clear, concise topic and typically run no longer than ten minutes. The series is one of the highest in demand among Canadian lawyers and is offered in a variety of file formats which make the episodes easily accessible regardless of location. Some examples of series topics include: "How to secure your laptop before crossing the border" and "Create a winning client retention strategy in five steps." The CBA is successful in its podcasting efforts because it pays attention to its audience, focuses on issues that affect their day-to-day life, and, as a result, links lawyers together Canada-wide.

Some of the most successful online shows feature niche-oriented content, such as advice for busy lawyers, but there are also many examples of companies reaching out to a mass audience, such as moms.

Whirlpool Home Appliances had a different approach when they started their podcast in 2007. The show, titled *American Family*, was hosted by former TV reporter Gigi Lubin, who interviewed people about family topics from caring for elderly relatives to the importance of mammograms to seeing a child off to college. The podcast barely ever mentioned Whirlpool products, was not promoted directly by the company's marketing team, and when it was only a year old it had tens of thousands of listeners. The company's aim was to reach out and relate to household decision-makers, without pushing their products.

Video Shows

In the summer of 2005, I ventured out to a small park near my G4TechTV office and launched what would soon become a staple on tech fans' iPods. With a small Mac laptop, an iSight Web camera, and some free video recording software, my friend and I shot our first episode of *commandN*. It was simply the two of us, along with my brother, sitting around talking about the latest tech news, which was something we were all undeniably passionate about. Although our initial production values were poor, we started to build a healthy fan base of dedicated viewers. One of those viewers, Brian McKechnie, offered to help us beef up the video and editing quality.

By the next summer, we routinely had one hundred thousand downloads per episode and were featured as a top video podcast in *Wired* magazine. Even more important to our audience, Karl Kerschl, a DC Comics artist for *Adventures of Superman*, drew a character in the series who was sporting a *commandN* jacket. We couldn't buy this type of exposure, which took place in an authentic way online. We continue to do the show today, with a group of viewers who have downloaded each show every week for years. After having won a number of awards and increasing the production values even further, we continue to base our success on the connection we have with our fans. Each week we share comments with them on the show's Web site, we routinely feature their feedback in the episodes, and we often showcase viewer videos. Creating a video show on the Web is getting less expensive than ever, making it a feasible part of many companies' social media strategy.

MOBILE TOOLS

Nestled in the Canadian Rockies, in the province of Alberta, is the lovely Kananaskis Resort. In the summer of 2009, I was heading there to speak to a group of broadcasters about how social media is affecting the news business. My drive up to the hotel from the airport should have been a quick hour or so, but thanks to a freak summer snowstorm it took me twice as long. En route, I also lost reception on my BlackBerry. My first impulse when I finally arrived in my room was to hook my computer up to the Internet with the hotel's Ethernet cable, just happy to be out of the snow and looking forward to getting caught up on some work. But this time, the bright blue cable staring out at me seemed like an unnecessary expense. After all, I had e-mail on my phone, and all the apps I could handle in one overnight trip. This was the first of many times since that I opted to use my handheld device instead of plugging in my computer, making me realize that the mobile world we are just starting to experience is going to change the way we communicate, consume, and connect forever.

Mobile Search

Mobile search is also one of the fastest-growing areas of smartphone use and there are many ways to employ the new iPhone,

BlackBerry, and Android phones' built-in GPS technology in apps. Imagine being able to inform customers of your new sale as they get close to your store. The best thing to do even if you're just getting your feet wet in the mobile space is to have your site tested for mobile compatibility. As mobile search becomes the norm you don't want people to navigate away from your traditional site just because it doesn't work properly on their phones.

Apps

Applications (apps), which are software downloads, are one of the greatest marketing tools a business can utilize in a mobile campaign. In December 2009, eMarketer released a study revealing that iPhone and Android users are spending more than half their mobile time using applications. Companies are following suit. Barnes & Noble, for instance, released a B&N bookstore application for the iPhone this year. B&N's app gives users access to millions of books at the touch of a finger. The app works like this. The user takes a photo of the book cover she is interested in, and seconds later, the user is sent all the information she could ever want about the book—including information about the book itself, the author, the publisher, and so on. More important, the app allows users to purchase or reserve a copy of the book right from the app. This innovative app is one of the top downloads of the year and continues to provide a great and simple useful tool for the user while promoting the B&N brand.

Marvel Comics legend Stan Lee released a neat iPhone app to

promote his new digital comic series *Time Jumper*, which is available for download through iTunes. The app, released in July of 2009, allows users to convert their digital photos to comic-book-style illustrations. Fan boys and girls are heavily using the app. It is simple, entertaining, and fully promotes the new series in a fun and innovative way.

Bank ING has released an extremely innovative—and free—T-Mobile G1 app based on "augmented reality." The ING Wegwijzer, which is the name of the mobile download, helps users locate the nearest ATM from where they are standing. What's great about this app is that it is capable of overlaying directions over real-time views of the surrounding area. For the users' benefit, ING has also developed a mini-site with instructions on how to install the software properly—for those new to the app world (this is an important ingredient to social media success: teach your audience exactly how to use the tools you're offering). This tool is of great use to the consumer and definitely increases brand awareness.

Nike's award-winning "Shoot Your Colors" campaign, although no longer running, serves as a prime example of how to do mobile marketing well. Nike gave away three thousand pairs of sneakers, from their Nike iD line, in a promotion that engaged the consumer in an innovative way. Users could take a photo of colors they found in real life—for example, graffiti on a building—and send it as a photo text to the promotional code number. Then Nike would send you a design for a customized pair of shoes based on the colors you sent in. In addition to this great idea, Nike had an immense interactive billboard in New York's Times Square where the consumer-based designs would be displayed on screen for thousands to see. Users loved the campaign and Nike sales soared. This campaign was a huge success because it was designed with the product and the consumer in mind. Nike's iD line of shoes centered on customization and so did the contest, accordingly. By engaging users and giving them results and exposure, it encouraged high levels of participation and word-of-mouth advertising.

QR Codes

When you walk down the street in Tokyo, there are flyers, posters, and billboards everywhere with bar codes front and center. Mobile phone users walk up to the codes, called QR codes, and scan them. Within seconds individuals have one-touch access to product information, contact information, and Web site addresses that they never have to type. While these modified bar codes look like little square pieces of art, they are actually hyperlinks that you can access if you have a QR-enabled reader on your phone. Most smartphones already have apps available for reading QR codes. These codes can link to a Web site or a social networking profile. They can even be used in place of concert tickets. The British pop band Pet Shop Boys released a video in 2007 with its own QR code that linked to a critique of the British national identity card concept that was being debated at the time.

It is up to manufacturers in Canada and the United States as to when this technology will come into widespread use in North America, but many analysts predict it will be soon.

SMS Messages

There are hundreds of examples of how SMS messages, also known as text messages, are at the centerpiece of many successful social media campaigns. Kraft Foods recently used SMS messages to promote a new brand of instant coffee. Consumers who opted in to receive messages on their phone (in other words, they weren't being spammed) got messages with a short code that allowed them to get a free sample of Jacobs (the new instant coffee). In total, Mobile Marketer (mobilemarketer.com) reported that Kraft received half a million requests for the sample. Additionally, more than eighty thousand users registered to receive future marketing correspondence from Kraft. The campaign was promoted primarily within a television commercial. Although many companies don't have budgets to produce mainstream media campaigns such as Kraft did here, there are inexpensive ways to leverage SMS messaging.

Ring Tones

Axe, which is always thinking up innovative marketing ideas, gained success with its original take on mobile marketing. The male body spray brand designed a "Little Black Book" app that gave away free ring tones to users. A ring tone is the audio that you hear when your phone rings. Many people, especially in the younger generation, like to customize this sound in an effort to personalize their mobile. Popular songs dominate the ring tone market, but Axe brewed up an idea to marry music to your address book. Using the app, fans could download specific songs they enjoyed and associate them with existing contacts (aka women). This campaign was successful because it was entertaining to the user and it got lots of attention online, all while reinforcing brand awareness and recognition.

WIKIS

"It's completely demented, is it not?" That's Wikipedia's co-founder Jimmy Wales in 2007 commenting to me in an interview about why the online encyclopedia, which is managed by an army of diehard fans (known as Wikipedians), actually works. After all, these people are not getting paid, but they are often devoting endless hours to ensure that each entry is as accurate as possible on a real-time basis. Yes, let's face it, there are so many reasons that Wikipedia shouldn't work, but instead volunteers have written more than 13 million articles on the site, making it a central destination for information of all kinds.

Remember my grandmother and her deep-seated fear of the Confederation Bridge in Charlottetown? As a demonstration, look up the "Bridge" entry on Wikipedia. Aside from the history of bridges and the types of bridges, there are also sections on bridge efficiency, movable bridges, a visual index, and differences and similarities in bridge structure. The visual index has more than a dozen categories, each with its own entry on Wikipedia. For example, the "Pigtail bridge" entry describes the bridge as "a type of road bridge, where the road curls and passes over itself." It also lists notable pigtail bridges, including one in Spain, one in Poland, and a few in the United States.

Wikipedia is also becoming a news source as entries are updated more quickly than news sites, despite fears of inaccuracy. Many critics complain about Wikipedia vandalism and the misinformation that can result. For example, rampant vandalism on Anna Nicole Smith's Wikipedia page in the days following her death caught the attention of traditional news media sources. Wales is dismissive of such criticism, telling me, "This actually shows how much the old media is completely on crack that anyone cares about Anna Nicole Smith. If it was a peace agreement in the Middle East, no one calls me."

Again, Wales's experience points to how many people continue to fear advances in online technology. Fortunately, on the wiki front, there are some companies who believe that collaborative technologies such as wikis are an important part of the future of their business.

Internal

A *wiki*, which is the Hawaiian word for "fast," is basically a Web site that anyone can edit, just like Wikipedia. In the business world, wikis can be a wonderful tool to share information and collaborate, especially inside an organization. Mobile phone giant Nokia estimates at least 20 percent of its 68,000 employees use wiki pages to update schedules and project statuses, trade ideas, edit files, and so on. "It's a reversal of the normal way things are done," Stephen Johnston told *BusinessWeek*. Johnston is a senior manager for corporate strategy at Nokia, who helped pioneer the technology. Where Nokia once bought outside software to help foster collaboration, now "some of the most interesting stuff is emerging from within the company itself," Johnston said. For many companies, using a wiki can also cut down on e-mails, since so much content can be managed within a wiki. Also, learning how to use a wiki is as simple as understanding how to use word processing software: just click and type. Better yet, wiki web-based software is very inexpensive, and a great way to keep a project moving along.

Walt Disney Co.'s Pixar studio used a wiki to manage production on one of its films. In fact, Pixar specifically attributes their success in releasing the 2008 film *WALL-E* on time to their wiki usage. The studio utilized a wiki to help coordinate new computerized animation tools. This sort of internal management is wonderful for keeping tabs on progress while keeping everyone in the loop. Although Pixar made a name for itself with its internal wiki usage, the company also has an extensive external wiki for the general public.

External

Do you know which Pixar movie was the first to show blood? You probably wouldn't guess it, but it's *Finding Nemo*, the story about the little clownfish that could. *Finding Nemo* also has an Easter egg cameo from another Pixar film: the dentist office waiting room in the film features a Buzz Lightyear toy on the floor. You can find this trivia and more nitty-gritty details about Pixar films on the Pixar Wiki, which is a comprehensive database for Pixar fans. This particular wiki contains hundreds of articles on a variety of topics. This is a place where people who love all things Pixar can come to discuss and share the smallest and largest details about the animation studio's work.

A Web design and development company called Red Ant in Sydney, Australia, utilizes a wiki as a collaboration hub for both employees and customers. The award-winning firm considers its collaborative workflow one of its greatest strengths; it allows all parties to add content easily and effectively. Red Ant enjoys the way its wiki enables clients and employees to interact on an all-encompassing level. It has improved relationships with clients and has encouraged a team mentality with employees. The wiki Red Ant uses is called Confluence, which, according to Red Ant, is the most straightforward wiki whose interface is easily presentable to clients. "We love that we can use Confluence across all of our business areas—to create a project space for a client to show them Flash game prototypes and design images, and then also to use it for detailed software documentation," says Red Ant managing director Ben Still on the Confluence Web site. In a situation like this, a wiki is great because it tracks and records all changes, so there is a detailed history of company and client conversations and feedback.

TOP FIVE SOCIAL MEDIA GADGETS

When I was speaking to a roomful of brand managers in Las Vegas in October 2009, I pulled out my Flip video camera on stage. I convinced the group to stand up with me and sing Kiss's 1975 hit "Rock and Roll All Nite." I shot the two-hundred-plus attendees belting out one line of this song over and over again. As fellow speaker Guy Kawasaki looked on, let's just say that it was a memorable conference moment. My purpose in asking the group to rise for a few minutes of fun was to demonstrate that there are opportunities everywhere around us to create compelling content to put online. Moreover, I wanted to showcase the power of my tiny little camera that never leaves my purse.

While your social media strategy will exist primarily on the Web, there are some great tech toys to push your plan forward with gusto. Here is a list of my top five social media gadgets. You don't necessarily need all of these, but depending on how you build out your strategy at least a couple of them will make your job easier.

1. Flip Video Camera

Most video cameras continue to get more and more complex, making it difficult to find that pesky record button. The Flip, on the other hand, has returned to simplicity. With just one bright red record button to get your shooting under way, the gadget is a must-have for any company building out a social media strategy with video as a component. Although the Flip is available in HD, to keep your file sizes reasonable the standard Flip is all you need. For less than $200, you might even want to get a few for your team. If you choose to do something requiring higher production value such as a regular Web video show, you will have to invest a little bit more money in a consumer video camera (one that allows you to attach an external audio input, which we'll talk about in a later chapter, so you can use mics to get the best quality).

2. Mobile Phone—iPhone vs. BlackBerry

Probably the most common gadget question I get these days is, BlackBerry or iPhone? Although I am a fan of many Apple products, I am a diehard BlackBerry user for no other reason than the user-friendly typing. As a social media user, I find there are decent BlackBerry applications that allow me to access both Facebook and Twitter on the go. However, Apple definitely dominates the mobile app world, so if you want a handheld device to get access to all the latest and greatest tiny pieces of software, the iPhone is the way to go. The BlackBerry, iPhone, and many other mobile devices allow you to take photos and videos, which should be an element of your strategy. Although the iPhone and BlackBerry are routinely fighting it out for mobile market share, Google's Android phone is also proving to be a contender. As Android devices start to grow in popularity, you will also see the app market for these phones explode (which could result in some serious competition for the iPhone).

3. USB Headset

For less than $50, a USB headset can save you a lot of money. This device looks like a large set of headphones with a prominent mic, which connects to your computer via a cord with a USB plug on one end. I recommend a USB-powered mic because it allows you to get great audio quality when you want to take business calls on Skype (a free piece of downloadable software that lets you make free phone calls over the Internet) or other voice-over-Internet technology. A headset is also a must-have if you plan to do an audio show online, as you can use it to record your voice directly into an audio editing program like GarageBand.

4. Digital Camera

Although a cameraphone is a handy little device to snap pics and post them online, a digital camera is a necessity for most social media initiatives to get some good quality photos that may later be used on your Web site or in other marketing materials. With prices dropping to just a couple of hundred dollars for a solid and compact still digital camera, you should keep this gadget handy when you have company events, travel to conferences, or spend time with key mavens in your industry.

5. Web Camera

Many computers these days come with a built-in Web cam. If you don't have one, you should pick one up. A Web cam will easily attach to a port on your computer to allow you to have video chat conversations via Skype. Not only does this open up a new way to hold meetings with individuals inside your organization, but a Web camera can also help you have video conversations with the people you friend online. If you choose to do a video podcast, a Web camera is a must.

Although this chapter broke down the top social media tools into specific categories, I can't stress enough how important it is that these tools are used together. Although you may not need all of them, they do work best in unison with each other. For example, if you decide that a podcast is right for you and you also want to blog, it's important that you post your podcast on your blog on a regular basis and also promote your blog address within your podcast. If you think that developing a mobile app is your best way to reach out and friend online, you should promote this app across all your marketing initiatives online (including your Web site). In fact, all of your social media initiatives should be tied into your company's Web site in some way. There is no need to build out a separate site to market these initiatives as they can be carefully rolled into your official online hub. For example, include your YouTube, Twitter, and other accounts on your "Contact Us" page so your audience knows that there are various ways to reach you. In turn, your official Web site should be the destination promoted on these various social media sites. We'll talk more about how to execute with these tools in chapter 6. Next up, it's all about your strategy.

Chapter five

The Strategy

In the 1989 movie *Field of Dreams*, Kevin Costner's character Ray hears a voice that whispers, "If you build it, they will come." All it takes is building a baseball diamond in the middle of an Iowa cornfield to bring in legendary players and thousands of eager fans. If only social media worked the same way. Unfortunately, that's not the case. It takes a lot of hard work to build a successful online presence and a trusted brand, and the only whispers you're going to hear may sound a lot more like angry complaints from an outspoken online community. Or, if you learn how to properly manage the conversation, they will be positive shout-outs about your company. For the business world, what happens online stays there, whether you like it or not, so you need to manage the conversation.

When I first started consulting and speaking in the social media space, I thought that managing a social media strategy was really quite simple, cut and dried, but after working with a

number of clients and talking with many marketing m⟩
I realized that there are so many layers to participating⟩
online space that it's no wonder companies get confuse⟩
overwhelmed. A lot of what's needed to make social media work
for you, aside from following the ABCs and knowing what tools
to use, is the commitment. Understanding that social media
isn't going away might convince you to develop a long-term plan.
After all, not only is social media changing the way we do business, it's also changing the way we interact outside of work. As a
McKinsey study pointed out, one in eight couples married in the
United States in 2008 met via social media. While I don't expect
you to get this close to all your colleagues and customers, it does
illustrate that social media is not just a fad. To help you manage
this new world, this chapter focuses on how to find the time and
resources, and why active listening is critical to making an
impact.

HOW TO FIND THE TIME

One of the most common questions I get following a keynote
presentation on social media is, "How do we find the time to
manage all of these online tools?" Audiences are often frustrated.
With so much work on their plates already, they can't imagine
piling on extra tasks, especially when it means using technology
that appears complex, confusing, and from their point of view,
possibly a royal waste of time.

When asked this question about time management at a real

estate conference where I was presenting, I reminded the audience that 80 percent of home buyers go to the Internet first to find information. Unlike years ago, they aren't calling up friends or driving around neighborhoods to find the best home fit (a quick real estate search paired with Google StreetView will do the trick). This often means that the vast majority of a real estate agent's customers only find him or her after they've found some homes that are of interest. In the real estate world, while home listings have come a long way and cater directly to the consumer, many agents are still not embracing the tools as quickly as the people they are trying to reach.

In this case, which is similar to many industries, when you decide not to participate in social media at all you are missing many opportunities to interact with your customers. Imagine if an ice cream truck driver decided to drive an empty country road instead of heading to streets filled with families living in the suburbs. After some time, that ice cream truck driver is going to have to pack it up and find another gig. With many industries like real estate, although it's still important to stick to some traditional ways of advertising, there has to be some effort to build out online marketing strategies so that you can be relevant to your consumers.

This doesn't mean that you need to devote eighty hours a week to social media, but you will have to make *some* time commitment. As I mentioned in chapter 3, the third rule in the ABCs of Internet friending is consistency. To get the results you want, it's important to start dedicating the time. Some companies find that just an hour a day is enough to get the ball rolling. Within one hour, you can easily write a quick update on Twitter, post a video to your blog, and search a number of listening tools discussed later in this chapter to find ways to participate in ongoing conversations.

Set up a process to check and update your social media accounts on a regular basis—make it a routine. For example, set aside an hour or so every morning for visiting social networking sites, checking e-mails coming in, and responding to any user feedback and requests. You should also spend part of this time finding new content to post on your accounts. The faster you develop some type of routine, the easier it will be to make sure you are covering as much social media space as possible. One of the best ways to develop a successful social media presence is to choose the social sites that make sense for your company's goals. If you try to manage dozens of accounts at a time, you will be spreading your efforts too thin if you don't have the resources to do it right.

As you build out your strategy, and if your organization can afford it, it often makes sense to dedicate one person to be in charge of all social media activities. This person then wears the community manager title within your company. If you want to build out your social media team even further, having a content creator is a good idea, as is someone on the technical support end to help you to manage the many technical issues that may arise.

However, if you can't afford multiple resources, one person

can easily wear these multiple hats. Or, alternatively, a couple of people within your organization can split up these responsibilities. When starting out, a small or one-person team who is charging ahead for your organization in the social media space is really all you need to make an impact, provided you follow the rules, develop a strong strategy, and execute it well.

Community Manager

The community manager is perhaps the most important position relative to your social media efforts (after the content has been written, of course)—he or she is both a community advocate and a brand evangelist, responsible for keeping your audience engaged and keeping the conversation relevant. The following are some important aspects of the community manager role:

Keep your ear to the blogosphere: Know what's being said about your organization online and be part of the online community. Keep tabs on your brand using Technorati.com, the popular blog search engine, and monitor other listening avenues such as Google Alerts (which allows you to track online buzz). There can be a lot of noise to get through to the important issues that may warrant special attention, so it's important that you don't just hear what's being said, but that you try to understand why it matters (and ask if you're not sure).

Connect and engage: Beyond just being part of the community, pursue stronger connections with key stakeholders and influencers both online and in the physical world. Let them know what's going on and discover ways to participate in what they have to offer. Listen to your audience and be part of the conversation. Think about what they are saying, respond thoughtfully to them, and discover ways to engage them. Present solutions to their problems as well as opportunities for them to provide more in-depth input. This will help to begin a valuable dialogue with your community.

Spread the word (but don't yell): As a key figure in the relationship between your audience and your social media efforts, your community manager can also be very helpful in promoting your organization and leveraging your social media tools to spread your message to the masses. It is exceedingly important that your community manager's evangelical responsibilities be conducted in a tactful, thoughtful, and respectful manner— with so many people complaining about information overload, you have to be sure that what you're transmitting is signal, not noise. Spreading the word about your efforts through the community can be accomplished to some degree simply by making sure your comments on external sites are labeled with your site name and address, and that the signature on your e-mails includes a reference to your company's blog or online community. By being tasteful and tactful, and by communicating openly and earnestly, the community manager can become a trusted member of the online community. However, this trust can be damaged much more easily than it can be built, so don't waste the opportunity for longer-term returns by pushing your message too hard and too explicitly online. Make people curious, don't push them to the door.

Respond (but only when necessary): Part of the reason you want to know what's being said about your brand online is so that you can intercept or otherwise deal with any significant issues as needed. You need to do this openly but tactfully, and only when necessary—you don't want to be seen as being thin-skinned or cutting off communications when anything critical is said. One of the great things about fostering a strong and connected online community is that the community itself can sometimes work in your defense without you needing to be involved. Try to determine what the issues are in problematic posts and objectively try to address them instead of defending them. It's important that you find the meaning behind the message, so check out related threads and do some research on who you are addressing and what their perspective may be. Above all, don't be defensive—be constructive.

Bring the message home: Because the community manager is exposed to so much information and feedback about the organization, he or she can be an important contributor to your company's future plans. Beyond simply monitoring what is being said online, a good community manager can delve deeper into the discussions to recognize common threads and to identify organizational strengths and liabilities from the perspective of the community. By bringing these messages back to the organization, the community manager is ensuring that your audience is heard. There are few things that can help build a healthy online community more easily than making participants feel like their comments actually count. This doesn't mean you have to follow every recommendation you get from your online community, but you do need to let them know that you're paying attention. In the end, all the input in the world doesn't mean much if it never results in any changes or improvements, and it is the community manager's role to make sure this message gets delivered to the decision-makers in the organization.

Community managers have a wide range of responsibilities. They must understand what your organization wants to accomplish online, and they should be experienced communicators, strategic thinkers, and people who are familiar and active in the online community. They are there to connect people, to maintain conversations, to make contributors feel welcome and valuable, and to serve as a liaison between the online community and your organization. The community manager should file regular (e.g., weekly or monthly) reports on community activities, including numbers of visitors and comments, but also quoting specific remarks, bringing attention to emerging trends in conversations or attitudes, and providing recommendations for next steps in the organization's online strategy. There are many tools to monitor online activity, which I'll discuss later. For example, I use bit.ly for all of my Web links. This service allows me to create a short URL that is easily shareable on social media sites. With bit.ly, not only can I find out how many people clicked on my link but I can also find out their geographic location and other important information.

Content Creator

The content creator, as the title implies, creates the content for publishing on your social media outlets. This role is essential for any level of social media endeavor. Not only must the content creator focus on presenting professional, Web-readable product, but he or she is usually responsible for coming up with story concepts and ensuring that content is geared toward the company's audience. The content creator may also be responsible for supplying graphical content for stories, whether that involves photographs, logo/design, tables, or other visual story elements. There are a few basic rules to being a good content creator:

Know the audience: It's important to be audience-focused if your goal is to increase readership and community interaction. Writing skills should be at an appropriate level for your audience and, even if content creators aren't involved in decisions about which specific stories they write, those stories must be reflective of what your audience is likely to be interested in. By incorporating these considerations into the writing, you'll be creating more valuable content for your readers.

Be professional: This is quite a catchall but it's important to never lose sight of who you're writing for (organizationally) and why. Most organizations will rightfully insist on well-written content that has been researched, respectfully written, thoroughly edited and spell-checked, and delivered on time—your audience will appreciate it too.

Be part of the community: Even if the community manager is the key person representing your organization in the community, find out how you can also be part of the discussion. Not only does having writers as part of the community help in answering direct questions about their stories, it also gives the audience a richer perspective on the people involved in your organization.

Write good stuff: Obviously the key role of a content creator is to write content, so write great content and remember that it is your audience who determines whether the writing is valuable. The content creator may or may not be supported by a dedicated content researcher or reporter (for collecting stories, conducting interviews, etc.), as well as a content editor and possibly a photographer/graphic designer (with responsibility for all visual aspects of a story, which may involve sourcing images in addition to creating them).

Technical Support

While everyone hopes their online ventures will proceed without any issues, unexpected problems need to be dealt with quickly and thoroughly. Technical support can help get your social media efforts up and running, and should make sure that your content management system and plug-in installs are up-to-date, and that the proper security is in place to ensure that your data is not compromised (this includes regular backups of stories and comments). Technical support may also be helpful in dealing with problematic uploads and, importantly, should be available to respond to any bug reports from visitors to your blog and other areas. This support need not be dedicated solely to the interactive community part of the organization, as issues are likely to be infrequent enough that a shared resource is sufficient.

Again, if you're only one person trying to manage your organization's social media efforts, it can be done. And it can be done effectively. The key for a one-person effort is to carefully decide how many online communities you can update and monitor. Try to find helpful tools on the Web that will allow you to cross-post on multiple sites. For example, there is a Twitter app listed among the applications on Facebook that will automatically post your most recent Twitter update as your Facebook status message (this can be very helpful when you are managing both accounts). If your social media initiatives are really successful, over time you may need additional help to respond more effectively.

TEN BEST PRACTICES TO SHARE WITH YOUR SOCIAL MEDIA TEAM

Whether you're a team of one or of many, there are some simple best practices that my company likes to share with clients to keep them on track. This list is something you'll want to keep in mind as you continue to expand in the social media space.

1. **Listening is the first step:** As in any conversation or relationship, it is difficult to realize the potential value if all you do is talk. Listen before you talk and give others a chance to speak as well. We'll go over this later in this chapter, along with the tools that will make the listening job easy to manage.

2. **Add value:** Again, the real world provides great insight here—don't talk just to talk, rather make sure that you are adding value to the conversation and providing your audience with information they are actually interested in (and you'll know what they're interested in by listening— see above). That's not to say that you have to totally avoid conversational or novel interactions, just make sure on the whole that you are providing value to your audience. Basically, talk with, don't talk at.

3. **Keep it human:** While your social media efforts may be centered around a business, social media interactions are centered around relationships between real people. Keeping the human connection is vital, so avoid overly formal, press release—type writing and don't be afraid to

show some personality (while still being polite and respectful). Talk to people, not specifically as customers or clients but rather as friends and associates. Acting human can also give your audience motivation to treat you in kind, whether that means forgiving some mistakes, not being too harsh in their comments or replies, and other responses that may not be the case when people deal with "faceless" corporations. For example, when creating an account on Twitter, use your company's name as the user name but make sure to include the name of the person who is actually managing this account in the bio.

4. **Be authentic, honest, and correct:** Authenticity relates somewhat to the previous point because you want to make sure that your audience can relate to, and believe in, what you say, and that as your relationship with your audience grows they can legitimately feel they are better getting to know both the people behind your company and the company itself. Remember the Domino's Pizza president? He spoke in real language. Avoid marketing-speak and keep in mind that misinformation can be passed around so quickly that it's often hard to correct an error after the fact, so make sure you do your fact checking up front. By the same token, it can often be very easy for people to do their own fact checking, so make sure what you post is honest and accurate, or you can expect that someone will point out your misinformation.

5. **Be consistent:** Within the ABCs of Internet friending at the beginning of this book, I mentioned consistency in

the context of an overall commitment to your social media work, but it also applies here on a more granular level. Whenever possible, use the same user name (and even user photo). Try to post with some regularity; don't blast out tons of posts and then remain silent for ages. Start slow and work up to it—it's better to increase your frequency than to decrease it as time goes on.

6. **Negative feedback is okay:** Take criticism as an opportunity to do better and try to identify the real problem. If it's something you can (and should) change then work on changing it. If it's something that you can't (or shouldn't) change then explain why. As I mentioned in chapter 2, on social media fears, many people are often afraid to hear the truth about their company, but hearing this and responding to it can only help your organization.

7. **Be part of the community:** Reach out to get other people involved in your activities and be involved in other people's activities as well. Write a guest blog post for someone else and have them write one for you. Comment constructively on other people's posts. In other words, don't just expect the community to care about what you have to say—you also have to care back. Recognize those who have made a contribution and link to them (and they'll likely return the favor). Create opportunities for community participation and participate in community activities yourself.

8. **Tell a story:** One of my clients, Canada Goose, has a fantastic advantage over most companies in that its prod-

ucts and evolution relate so strongly to so many great stories. With a fifty-year family history making outdoor wear for extreme conditions, the company's stories about how their coats have protected everyone from royalty to celebrities in all types of climates are endless. While a blog, for example, is a much easier place to provide the background and context to tell a great story, you can still leverage tools like Twitter to link to these kinds of posts and share stories with your audience across different platforms. Keep in mind that your audience probably has their own stories to tell as well, so give them the opportunity to do so. Stories are memorable, poignant, and form a major part of our cultural history, so be sure to leverage storytelling in your social media activities.

9. **Make a commitment:** If you are becoming more active in the social media sphere, show that you mean it by properly allocating resources (mostly people and time) to this pursuit. Your audience will appreciate having one or more people who are dedicated and involved in your social media activities whom they can address, and you may find that your efforts will be ineffective if your involvement is primarily ad hoc. Social media can easily be a team effort. In fact, as we've seen from the Zappos example, it can often be beneficial to have your entire organization commit to participating in this space so that on a larger scale you can engage in more conversations. Take a look at the Twitter page on the Zappos Web

site (twitter.zappos.com). There are so many things that they do right here. For example:

- **Zappos Public Mentions:** This is a feed pulled from Twitter that lists any time someone uses the word *Zappos* in a message.
- **Employee Tweets:** This feed pulls in the live Twitter feeds of hundreds of Zappos employees who are more than happy to share their love for their employer with the world.
- **Employee TwitPics:** This is a feed of photos that Zappos employees are posting on Twitter.
- **Employees Who Twitter:** This is a list of the approximately five hundred Zappos employees who are on Twitter.
- **Other Brands on Zappos.com:** This is a list of partner Twitter accounts, such as Adidas and Converse Kids, which shows Zappos's support for its business community.
- **Beginner's Quick Start Guide and Tutorial to Using Twitter:** Written by Zappos's CEO, this is a simple how-to note to get Zappos's customers familiar with the micromessaging site, including how to effectively get Twitter help if you need it.

10. **Track your accomplishments:** If you are making the kind of investment you should be in social media, then be sure to monitor and evaluate your accomplishments. A

monthly report outlining your number of Twitter followers, Facebook fans, blog traffic, comments, RSS feed subscribers, conversation tracking, sales/inquiries resulting
from social media activities, and other metrics not only
lets you see how you're doing, it can be very important
in justifying continued resource allotment to these
activities by demonstrating your "Return on Engagement" (ROE). This is the one piece that often gets left
out of social media strategies, but remember that the
Internet has better tracking tools than any other communications platform. In other words, take advantage of
the tools that exist to help you along.

Comanaging Accounts

As I mentioned above, it can help to have more than one person
involved in your social media work. Companies such as Black-
Berry are doing this now using personnel initials to indicate who
at the company is tweeting (but I prefer first name/title, e.g.
Amber/Sales). BlackBerry, also known as @BlackBerryHelp on
Twitter, has photos of its social media team members on its
account page, along with a note about each member's favorite
food (a nice touch to humanize the tech company's brand). Also,
as discussed in chapter 4, there are some excellent tools out there
to manage multiple online accounts. When comanaging is done
properly there are also some significant advantages:

Less work: Power friending takes a lot of effort, so you need to be on top of every tweet, Facebook request, YouTube comment, and more. Sometimes this level of participation is too much for one person. Splitting the workload not only takes the stress off one person, but it also encourages internal conversations on these various online platforms within your team. Again, friending from the inside out is the number-one best way to make your social media strategy a success. Once these tools become an integral part of the way your organization communicates internally, your external social media strategy will become an organic extension of this approach.

More variety: When just one person is managing your online presence, that person's opinion is the only one that will get shared on the Web. While this does help to get across a consistent message, it can be beneficial to have one person, the community manager, monitor online conversations but have multiple people contributing content. Chances are that within your organization there are a wide variety of interests among your team members, just as there is in the outside world. Actively showcasing these different interests can help you to build up your community online since you'll be able to reach out to more people in an authentic way.

More friending: As of July 2009, Facebook reported that eight million users become fans of pages every single day (up from 2.5 million at the beginning of 2009). When your organization sets up a Facebook page, imagine how beneficial it will be if more than one person within your organization promotes that page. Each person on Facebook around the world has approximately 150 friends in his or her particular network, so if you can engage a team of people at your company to reach out and friend within their own networks you will grow your community exponentially. This is powerful word-of-mouth marketing.

If your company does go the route of comanaging accounts, keep in mind that you should be open about this to the community at the other end. Again, signing off on messages with your name can be a good way to demonstrate that social media is a team effort. You can also put a page up on your Web site or blog that lists the specific names of your social media team, and their respective departments, so individuals can feel free to reach out to the person who best suits their needs when looking for more information or help from your organization.

THE FULL MONTY AT FORD

Scott Monty is the head of social media at Ford Motor Company. He is a great example of how to integrate personality into corporate branding. He has nearly 28,000 followers on Twitter who receive his daily perspectives on all things related to social media. He writes a popular blog that thousands of people visit each day where he provides in-depth content about online marketing.

At Ford, he serves as the face of the company in the public light. He maintains the company's Twitter account, Facebook page, and so on. Monty's unique role at Ford is to provide customers with content they could otherwise not access. For example, Monty will interview Ford CEO Alan Mulally as he exits a meeting, asking the questions users have sent in via Twitter or e-mail—and Monty will update Twitter post answers in real time. Monty believes, especially with traditional corporate business, that social media is a wonderful and inspiring way to humanize a brand—and Monty is doing just that.

On the blog front, Monty realizes that nearly everyone drives. Among this immense group, there is a lot of diversity in interests, values, and needs. This is why he—and his team—blog about issues indirectly related to the company but directly related to the user. Building brand awareness through covering issues like fuel efficiency for the green consumer, or safety issues for moms, is Monty's specialty.

Monty is also responsible for the popular Ford Fiesta Movement campaign, which allowed one hundred people chosen by Ford to try out the Ford Fiesta for six months, uploading videos and posting about their experiences with the product.

Monty credits the success of his efforts at Ford to being in the right place at the right time. Ford came out on top of the big three during the downturn of 2008, when it was the only major U.S. auto manufacturer not to take government aid, thanks to a massive transformation that was already under way within the company. Monty himself was already well established as a name within the social media space and had worked with Ford to develop a cohesive plan. "A solid social media strategy meant that we had a plan and were well prepared for the newfound attention we received," he told me. "Social media has allowed

Ford to break through the clutter and become more human—taking risks, being on the cutting edge, and having a voice in an otherwise commoditized world. . . . At Ford, we take social media seriously. It's more than a hobby or a fad for us. It's transforming the way we do business."

Monty's effect on Ford customers is tangible; here's just one example, taken from the blog of Edward Boches:

> Yes, Scott Monty gets too much press, but he is the best example of a staid, stodgy old brand (Ford) becoming a human I somewhat care about. Dammit, if my wife needs a new minivan, I will feel guilty now if I do not test drive a Ford. (And from a Toyota family, that is a revelation.)

SIT BACK AND LISTEN LARGE

One of Monty's jobs is also to listen to what customers are saying, and then provide feedback and information as necessary. Just take a look at Monty's Twitter account, @scottmonty, and you'll quickly find that he spends more time listening and responding to people online than he does simply broadcasting his own messages. There is a slide in a popular YouTube video called "Social Media Revolution" that says it best: "Successful companies in social media act more like Dale Carnegie and less like David Ogilvy. Listening first, selling second." Listening can also lead to some creative social media ideas.

When I interviewed the founders of Etsy, which is an online

home for hundreds of thousands of craft buyers and sellers from more than 150 countries, Rob Kalin brought up a story about how keeping an eye on what the site's visitors were searching for kept their strategies in check.

"I remember when a month after we first launched the site the top referral words were from search engines and one of them was *amigurumi*," Kalin said. "So I searched and there were about twenty amigurumi dolls. We decided to have a contest to encourage others to make these for the site." An amigurumi doll is a crocheted doll or toy, which originated in Japan. If you visit Etsy today, you'll find a number of these crafts available for sale on the site. Although Kalin didn't originally know what an amigurumi doll was, he quickly realized that if his community was searching for this item then he ought to know more about it fast.

Listening is key to connecting with and improving your online community. With careful listening (discussed further in the next chapter), you too can effectively respond to the needs of your customers.

RESOURCE YOUR STRATEGY, FROM THE INSIDE OUT

When launching your social media strategy, the temptation is to join a slew of popular networking sites and start broadcasting (aka shouting) your message to the outside world. However, some of the most effective social media strategies start at home (or, more specifically, inside your own organization). Your company's employees are often your best brand ambassadors. Many of them may already be participating on the sites you plan to use, and they can help to carry your company's conversations to their own networks, increasing your marketing reach. Too many companies fail to communicate their social media presence from the inside out. To encourage social media adoption and sharing from within, here are a few key strategies to bring your whole team on board.

E-mail Signatures

These are a tiny little piece of marketing heaven. Although Nielsen Online stats from the end of 2008 show that social networking is more popular than e-mail, the average business person continues to send and receive hundreds of e-mails a day. When you're trying to promote your new online presence to the outside world, one of the best places you can start is in your signature. Include your Twitter, Facebook, YouTube, and other social media links in your e-mail footer. When recipients receive a message from you, they can now easily friend you on any applicable social networking Web sites. This is a free and easy way to build community online.

Team Twitter

Whether you have a team of three people or three hundred, when you decide to launch a social media marketing plan, inform the other people in your organization. Other team members can be the best messengers for your brand online. When you include your plans in company meetings, everyone can be a part of the strategy. Now employees will know where to find official accounts and you can also let them know how they can contribute to your efforts. Also, don't forget that there are some amazing online tools that can be used to build community within an organization, such as wikis, blogs, and more.

Comment Crawls

Remember when you were at a dance in junior high school? No one wanted to be the first person on the dance floor, so students crowded back against the gym walls. The same applies to social media. No one wants to be the first person to comment, so they stay away until the conversation gets going. Don't let this happen to your blog, Facebook page, or other social sites online. There is nothing wrong if people within your organization are the first to post comments, photos, videos, and more. In other words, make the first move so it's easy for your community to participate.

Facebook Pages

Facebook pages are simple to set up and can link you and your company to the millions already using the site (but, like any social media initiative, someone on your team needs to work to seed the page with information and encourage conversation). They can also function as a platform to organize meet-ups, source feedback, send messages to your fans, and rally around similar ideas and solutions to problems. Your Facebook page is your company's profile on the world's largest social networking Web site. Ask your employees to join your official Facebook page, which will help to increase exposure from the inside out. After a page is set up on Facebook, you may also want to consider participating in Facebook groups (where you can't market directly like you can on your own page, but you can participate in brand-related conversations and drive members to your Facebook home). A Facebook page is free to create.

Community Talks

Share your knowledge and expertise with your community. Build up your brand and your authority as a leader in your field by extending your personal reach, well, in person. This is an opportunity to take the online experience offline. There are probably dozens of local business workshops and events in your city on a monthly basis (such as tweet-ups, which are events organized on Twitter) where you can share your organization's internal culture and expertise. For example, my company does a lot of online video production and podcast creation for clients so our video producers, Jeff and Chris, are active at community events such as PodCamp where hundreds of individuals gather in cities across

North America to learn about how to create good online content. This is a great way to not only network but sell yourself, your organization, and your insights.

Linking In

Although LinkedIn is often considered a destination to find employment, the site also offers a free opportunity to connect and explore others in your field or area of expertise (inside and outside your organization). There are also some wonderful tools on LinkedIn that people never actively use. There are dozens of groups that offer a way to communicate with other LinkedIn members to help answer questions and solve problems. Go in and give help when you can and ask for it when you need it. If there is no group that fits your needs, start one and chances are others will appreciate and participate in it. The "recommendation" feature, which allows others to give you a public referral, is high on the list of valuable LinkedIn features and can be a great way to build credibility for your own brand or your company's services. Feel free to ask your colleagues to recommend you, and return the favor with your own recommendation for them. As with commenting in other blogs, honesty and transparency go a long way in the LinkedIn world. Recently, LinkedIn has added a feature so that you can post a status update on your profile, similar to what is available on a Facebook personal page. As of February 2009, comScore, which is a marketing research company, revealed that

LinkedIn is one of the top twenty social networking Web sites in the United States with almost seven million visitors a month.

TIME FOR A PLAN

With the rules of Internet friending fresh in your mind, it's time to sit down and start laying the foundation for your strategic plan. Yes, your plan. Too often businesses start the friending process without any sort of strategy in place. Although it's easy enough to launch a profile page on YouTube or sign up for a Twitter account, without a strategy in mind you will never be able to see the benefits of playing to win in this space. To get the best results from your plan, commit for at least six months.

Currently, I'm working with a client on a three-year social media strategic plan. What this does is to give a business the time it needs to build up community online. After all, social media, as I've said many times before, is here to stay. According to eMarketer, between 2006 and 2009 the number of people using social media grew from 17 percent of Internet users to 26 percent of Internet users (as the total number of Internet users exploded around the world). With continued growth the majority of Internet users will be relying on social media over the next decade as an invaluable communications avenue. By the end of this book, you will have the knowledge you need to develop your social media strategy, from the rules, to tools, to maintenance, to budgeting. As you build this strategy, there are a few overall guidelines to get you pointed in the right direction.

Create a Listening Plan, and Follow It

After a flight to Chicago in 2008, Dave Carroll, from the band Sons of Maxwell, quickly wished he had driven to his destination. When he arrived at O'Hare, his neighbor on the plane noticed that the United Airlines baggage handlers were tossing around a guitar. Carroll's heart sank when he discovered that his expensive Taylor guitar had been badly damaged by the ground crew. The musician proceeded to send United a number of e-mail complaints, but the airline did not accept full responsibility for Carroll's loss. Instead, United offered the singer a small bit of compensation for his damaged guitar. Prior to the Internet, this story of poor customer service would have ended here. However, this was not the case.

Carroll joined together with some friends and created a music video called "United Breaks Guitars." The YouTube hit depicts careless baggage handlers and United employees who appear to turn their back on their customers. The song racked up nearly four million views in the first ten days alone and led to a number of mainstream media appearances. It's difficult to put a dollar amount on the cost of negative publicity to United, but the PR hit they took was huge to say the least.

When first kicking off your strategic plan, include a section on your listening plan. Companies that are successful in the social media space not only know how to interact, they also know how to follow along with conversations that are taking place online. Ten years ago we had to rely on a search engine, such as Google, to listen to conversations online, but today there are a number of excellent tools to make this process a whole lot easier, which we'll cover in more detail in chapter 6.

Tap into Existing Networks

While you might think you're the first mover in the social media space in your particular industry, chances are that's not the case. Many millions of networks already exist online, from e-mail newsletter lists to online forums to private Twitter groups. Just because you've finally decided to come to the social media party today doesn't mean it hasn't started already. Keeping this in mind, take some time to research where your target audience is already spending time online. Join these communities. Participate in conversations. Draw upon what you think works and what doesn't work to build out your company's social media strategy. As you start to develop your own online spaces, you will be in a good position to invite the people whom you've met on the Web along the way.

Find the Key Mavens in Your Industry

Now that you know how to play nice, let me tell you who to play nice with. Although at first there might appear to be value in collecting thousands and thousands of friends, for most companies it's important to also focus on establishing relationships with key mavens in their industry. Throughout this chapter I will discuss how to build up a mass of Internet friends, but also how to ensure you're connecting with the right people to ensure the successful building of your brand.

Chris Reid at Yamaha went to where his customer community lived online to find out what they were saying. This kind of engagement is key, but before you head outside to find your community, friend from the inside out. For example, Best Buy looked within their own company for key maven feedback. More than twenty thousand Best Buy employees are currently members of Blue Shirt Nation, an online community where employees can openly talk and listen to one another about how to improve customer service and marketing at the electronics chain. As for measuring the success of this community, Best Buy marketing executives highlight a video contest they supported on Blue Shirt Nation to boost 401(k) enrollment. Thanks to the strong community within the company's internal social network, 401(k) enrollment increased 30 percent. It was employees who originally started this network, but management quickly realized its value and supported it 100 percent. In other words, Best Buy knew that it was important to play nice with its thousands of employees to build its brand reputation.

Own Your Space, Even If You're Not There Yet

There are hundreds of social media Web sites online. With such a wealth of options, it's easy to feel overwhelmed. When you kick off your plan, your strategy should include selecting three or four social media Web sites that are a good fit for your organization. Although this means that you will only actively participate in a small number of places online, you should still consider registering your brand in a dozen or so places so that you have the option to expand your plan. In the late 1990s many individuals would squat on certain domain names, and the same is happening right now in the social media space. In other words, even if you're not actively using the top social media Web sites it makes sense to register your company on these sites now so you have the option to use these tools for your brand in the future. There is a helpful service online called Namechk. This service will allow you to find out if your desired brand name is available across multiple social media Web sites. Within seconds you'll be able to determine if your online brand name will work for your social media initiatives or if you need to get a little more creative. Remember, it's important to maintain the same name when you register social media accounts so that you ensure consistency.

THE OBAMA MACHINE

My friend Rahaf Harfoush worked as a volunteer on President Barack Obama's social media campaign. She regularly makes the point that the Obama campaign clearly highlighted how effective social media can be when it is integrated into an organization's strategy (as opposed to adding social media on as an afterthought). While most companies do not have Obama budget's ($639 million in overall funds to be exact) when putting together an Internet friending strategy or the resources to manage such a campaign (35,000 volunteer groups), every company has the ability to execute a clear strategic vision for managing a community of friends on a daily basis. In short, Obama's team followed all of the guidelines outlined above—creating a listening plan, and following it; tapping into existing networks; finding the key mavens; and owning his space.

In a recent e-mail, Harfoush explained to me why she thinks social media is increasingly a desired way to connect:

> Social media allows you to form connections with a community of people who share the same interests as you. You can easily keep track of a wider network which provides endless opportunities to share experiences, knowledge and build relationships. I have learned more from my online network of friends in one month than I learned in school in four years! I have looked to my online friends for troubleshooting, suggestions and advice on just about every conceivable topic and they have never let me down.

In November 2008 eMarketer.com released a report about social media marketing. More than 85 percent of the U.S. marketing executives questioned agreed that customer engagement is the most important benefit of using social media marketing. Sixty-five percent of executives cited direct customer communications as a benefit and almost 60 percent said learning customer preferences was another direct advantage. Respondents also noted that social media marketing provided low cost and brand-building benefits, something that is not always easy to measure.

MEASURING SUCCESS: RETURN ON ENGAGEMENT (ROE)

One of the biggest mistakes I see companies make when they first start to consider social media to grow their brand is expecting an instant and measurable return on investment (ROI). If you think that building relationships online is going to immediately result in profit, you should reset your expectations. Within this chapter I will further outline how to find the resources to manage your social media initiative and how you can do so in a cost-effective manner.

As for measuring results, in September 2009, a Mzinga and Babson Executive Education survey found that 86 percent of professionals across a variety of fields are experimenting with social media. Out of that group, only 16 percent are measuring ROI. Most respondents admitted that they didn't even know that it was possible to measure anything accurately in the social media world. For the purpose of social media, it's better to focus on return on engagement.

There are so many ways to measure social media initiatives,

but you need to first decide what your goals are. These goals can be divided into two categories: qualitative and quantitative. On the qualitative side, this involves feedback that you're getting online, participation in various social media campaigns, and general conversations that are coming back your way. On the quantitative side, the Internet provides a number of fantastic tools to monitor your work and track your success. Whether your goal is to build up a community of a thousand people on Twitter or to grow your blog traffic to fifty thousand visitors a month, the technology exists to help you reach those numbers— just make sure that every month you track your progress in this space. If you're really looking for evidence of return on investment as a dollar amount, here are some ways that companies are benefitting financially.

Some social media tools are simply good for sharing information in a cost-effective way. For example, a wiki, which is an online document or site that anyone can edit, is an excellent way to create an online collaborative hub for internal and external sharing. If your organization is building a Web site, a wiki can be a valuable way to keep track of all of the design and content changes, allowing all users to see and track changes. While you may not see a direct return on investing in this type of tool, there is a benefit to leveraging this technology. Instead of having to create and print elaborate marketing materials, you can often create a wiki for free, such as MediaWiki, which is very popular in the non-profit world (for a minimal charge, services such as

PBworks also integrate social networking tools). Not only is there a cost-saving benefit, but wikis allow for easy and effective engagement within your organization.

Some social media tools can put an extra bit of money in your company's pocket. The biggest growth area we're seeing now, which I will also expand on in the next chapter, is the exploding world of mobile applications. Since consumers are often prepared to pay for downloads, such as iPhone applications, this can be a source of revenue for your company. Although many apps are offered online for free, paid apps are also very much the norm. Virgin Atlantic, Richard Branson's hip airline, launched an iPhone app for $4.99 that aims to help its customers who have a fear of flying. The download, which comes complete with videos to show the mechanics of a routine landing and takeoff, also generated an enormous amount of press when it launched (which can be seen as the equivalent to millions of dollars in advertising for the airline).

Some social media tools help you to offer discounts to your best customers. Foursquare, which is a mobile tool that allows users to share their exact location with friends, also has a vibrant social gaming component. As a user frequents a certain destination more than anyone else on the service, he is crowned "mayor" of that location. With information like this, companies can now easily pinpoint who is buying or using their products and offer these individuals special treatment. If the engagement with these customers is positive, this brand evangelist has the power to market your products to their network.

The examples above are just a few simple ways to demonstrate how social media strategies done right can offer a substantial return on engagement (and investment). The next chapter is all about how to leverage the tools we've already discussed, and execute in an effective way.

Chapter six

The Execution

Before you start communicating on the Web, you need to stop, search, and buy. Whether you plan to use your organization's name or a marketing campaign title as an online destination for all your social media efforts, register the address online using a domain provider such as GoDaddy (just one of a number of providers). This is different than owning that name on a site such as Facebook, which is free. A domain name will cost you approximately $10 per year, a small expense for an important branding opportunity.

I'll wait . . .

It goes without saying that a great domain name is key to starting off on the right foot. The next thing to do is to put your plan on paper and pick your weapons. Test out some of the powerful Web-based tools mentioned in this book before you try building something from scratch (which is often expensive and time-consuming).

When I started working in the Web world I was a community manager for an e-procurement company in San Francisco. My job was to manage a team of eight people who provided educational purchasing information to colleges and universities. We, like many companies in the late 1990s in the Bay Area, had received a good chunk of investment money, so we dumped tens of thousands of dollars into building our own social media technology. Early in 2000, if you wanted to design and develop technology such as online forums or wikis, where individuals could converse, designers were expensive, developers cost even more, and as project management fees dragged on, it was difficult to justify the expense.

Today, online tools are dramatically less expensive. In fact, many tools are free or require just a small monthly fee. For this reason alone, there is really no need to invest thousands of dollars in creating your own customized online tools. The drain on your time and resources is not worth it. Furthermore, since Web development is outside the core competency of most businesses, there is no point in competing with the production speed of third-party tools that are available today. For example, Wordpress is a free blogging and social media platform that is excellent for a range of organizations, from a small non-profit looking for a simple online presence to an international media outlet publishing breaking news around the clock. Instead of rolling your own tools, your valuable dollars should be spent on content creation and on purchasing some of the hardware needed to make yourself heard *and* seen.

In the summer of 2007, toy company Mattel launched The Playground Community, a private online space for five hundred mothers. That fall, Mattel announced a worldwide toy recall. Each day Mattel spokespeople communicated directly with the moms in this group to determine how they should deal with the recalls and what feedback the community had about their actions. Despite the recalls, fourth-quarter 2007 sales were up 6 percent over the previous year and Mattel's agency, Communispace, was granted a Forrester Groundswell Award in the "Listening" category for doing the right thing with a community of customers online. The feedback on the program was overwhelmingly positive. Mattel's online customers responded with glowing comments like this:

> I think it shows that Mattel really has been listening to participants in [the community] and parents around the country. I like that he [Mattel CEO Bob Eckert] was specific about what Mattel plans to do. And I felt he was honest and sincere. It made me feel that they're not going to hide anything from us, but will continue to be up front.

There are many Web-enabled tools you can use to easily create a community (like the Mattel example) that can be the foundation of your online marketing efforts. All it requires is the proper execution. The rest of this chapter gives you some detailed guidance on actually executing your social media strategy.

BLOGS

Blogging initially defined what social media and Web 2.0 buzz was all about, and blogs are even more relevant today. It's your voice, your printing press telling the world what you think and where you or your company are headed. It's incredibly easy to get your blog up and running on services such as Blogspot, Typepad, Squarespace, or any of the other blogging platforms that are already popular on the Web. This is a cost-effective way (in fact, it costs nothing or just a nominal fee, such as $8 per month for Squarespace) to test the waters, build community, and gauge response and effectiveness without building a large expensive platform. If your blog takes off and you need more capabilities, you might want to hire a designer and developer to build a custom site, but you need to focus on building your audience first.

Here are some tips and workflows you can incorporate to build your blog into a popular destination.

Content

Idea it: The lifeblood of blogs is the stories and ideas that you share with your audience. Creating content over and over again can seem like a daunting task at first, but a little brainstorming and a good inventory of what you and your team think is interesting. Similarly, what you have questions about may yield more content than you can handle. One of the best ways to generate new ideas is to ask yourself what problems you've had with some aspect of your industry.

Research it: Authenticity and honesty make great bedfellows and are essential to any story, digital or not. A poorly researched piece will reflect negatively not just on you, but on your organization, and it is much harder to get rid of an unfavorable association with your blog than a positive one.

Write it: People read differently on the Web. We have a tendency to scan the page quickly and look for keywords or links of interest. You can take advantage of this tendency by writing more easily scannable articles:

- Write titles and headings that describe your post. They should convey the content of the blog entry—don't try to be cute or make your title into a teaser (Twitter is the place for creative titling, not the blog itself). For example, opt for something clear and informative like "Gas tax increased 10%" instead of the more cryptic and punny "Tax changes not a gas." The more accurate you are with the blog title, the better chance there is for someone to find the post via a simple search.
- Use lists. If your information can be broken into point form (bulleted where order is irrelevant, numbered where order is important), that's all the better for the eager scanner.
- Use digits instead of letters for specific numbers, for example, "24" not "twenty-four." Conventional writing rules

don't apply, as users need to be able to see the numbers at a glance.

- Link if you can. Make the link text reflect what will be at the site if you click on that link. Try to say, "click here to find out more about issue A and why it matters to you" rather than, "click here for more info."

- Put keywords in titles and text. This will help search engines find your posts as well as informing the reader what the content is about quickly. These can be highlighted links, boldface, italics, etc.

- Use the inverted pyramid. Put your important information at the top and work your way down the post with the less important information following. Put only one idea into each paragraph. Economy of words is very important on the Web and will allow readers to quickly jump from paragraph to paragraph.

- Be concise. The clearer your writing, the more successful your post will be.

Credibility

As I mentioned in chapter 3, "The Rules," authenticity is key. If you have a well-written, well-researched blog post that teaches readers something it will be passed around the community and can serve as a lightning rod for discussion. For example, Scott Monty, who I mentioned earlier, is in charge of social media efforts at Ford Motor Company. As an avid blogger, he educates Ford fans about what is happening with various campaigns and how individuals are helping to push his company's brand forward. In a holiday post around Thanksgiving 2009, Monty thanked his community of people who have made his job easier, and Ford's brand more successful. In an authentic voice, he shared results from an initial online marketing campaign that yielded more than six million YouTube video views and almost seven hundred thousand Flickr photo viewers, and he revealed how these initiatives helped to raise awareness of a new Ford vehicle (the Fiesta) to 58 percent. He went on to mention how all the buzz cost $0 in traditional advertising.

Consistency

There is a lot of chatter in the blogging world regarding when and how often to blog. Although there are no clear-cut guidelines or set-in-stone rules, you should be consistent with whatever schedule works best for you, your organization, but most important, your audience. Whatever your publishing schedule, keep the blog fresh. Nothing will nullify your commitment to the new school of communication as much as an old, rarely updated blog. Also note that posts do not need to be long to be good, they just need to have useful information. It may be that a single post consists of only two hundred characters but includes links to other valuable information and an explicit call to discussion. In both of the above cases, it can be helpful to "seed" your comments thread by starting off the comments discussion; you can add additional information or links and a stated viewpoint to encourage more comments and a focused discussion.

In addition to writing original posts and essays, there are many other ways to share content and keep people coming back to your blog. You can embed video, audio, photos, or other content (always linking to the content source), with your own description of this media and why it's interesting. This can include your analysis and opinion or just something you liked that you thought you'd share with your readers.

MICROMESSAGING

Twitter is a free social networking and micromessaging service that enables its users to send and read messages. Tweets, which I described earlier, are text-based posts of up to 140 characters displayed on the author's profile page and delivered to the author's subscribers, who are known as "followers." Senders can restrict delivery to those in their circle of friends or, by default, allow open access. Users can send and receive tweets via the Twitter Web site, Short Message Service (SMS), or external applications.

When you start to "tweet" you'll need to know a few terms to get you going . . . for instance, "tweet" is a verb or it can be used as a noun to describe a message on Twitter. Here is more on Twitter terminology.

Tweet: A message/update posted on Twitter.

Following: What you do to another Twitter user/person/company to get the messages they post on Twitter to show up on your Twitter timeline/home page. When someone follows you, they see your messages. A list of who you are following is available at the lower right of your Twitter home page.

@username: A way to both identify a Twitter user and to direct your tweet at a given individual. You can initiate a "Public Reply" (i.e. an @username reply) by typing the "@username" text at the beginning of your message manually or by clicking on the Public Reply "curved arrow" that you will see when hovering over a tweet on your Twitter feed. (It is very important, especially for businesses, to regularly check incoming @username mentions and reply as necessary, as these are conversations/remarks about your company and customers. Depending on the nature of the tweet they may expect a reply from you.)

DM (Direct Message): This is a way to privately message another user without it appearing on your public timeline. It's a little like e-mail and you can adjust the settings to actually have Twitter e-mail you each time you receive a DM. Keep in mind that both parties need to be following each other for direct messages to be sent.

RT (Retweet): It is now an official Twitter command (the company added this feature after watching how prevalent it became among its users). When you click retweet on a message, it places a RT at the beginning of your tweet and has become the standard way to note that you are forwarding on someone else's tweet (so that you give them the credit). This is a good way to show appreciation for, and to share, other people's content. You will occasionally also see users who, with the same "retweeting" purpose, instead place "(via @username)" at the end of the tweet.

Shortened URLs: Because of the brevity of the 140-character limit in Twitter, many users find it advantageous to use shortened URLs so that they have more space to say what they want in their tweets (as URLs can take up a lot of characters without adding any value)—www.tinyurl.com is just one example of a URL shortening service, and allows you to customize the shortening to some degree. However, with the popularity of social media sites where links are shared in small spaces, services such as bit.ly allow users to shorten URLs but they also add increased functionality to track clicks, revealing information such as popular traffic times and users' geographic location. This information is invaluable as you monitor your online conversations.

Hashtag (#): A pound (#) symbol followed by a term is a way to roughly categorize messages in Twitter. Since there are no standard topics, often users utilize the hashtag from a previous post that their new tweet relates to—companies in particular tend to take advantage of this. Essentially, this just facilitates search when the direct search term is not elsewhere in the tweet. For example, "Want to win free seats to the next show? Just DM me #JakesJazz."

Trending Topics: The most-mentioned terms on Twitter at any given moment are updated continually as Trending Topics, showing what users are talking about most. Trending Topics can be found just above the "Following" area to the lower right of your Twitter home page.

Tweet-up: An in-person gathering organized (although not necessarily exclusively) via Twitter.

Lists: These are separate timelines that you customize your-self that can include your coworkers, industry-specific people, your family members, or anyone else you want to separate from your public timeline and categorize. If you're looking for ideas in terms of who to follow when you first sign on to Twitter, checking out a user's lists is a great way to build up your own community.

Now that you know some basic Twitter lingo, here are some tips on how to use this tool:

Have an informative bio section on Twitter: One of the first places any potential follower will look for information about you is in your Twitter bio. Be sure to include your name, a link to a Web site, and a bio that is informative and concise. Phrases like *adventurer to the extreme, Ninja,* or *star-fighter pilot* are cute, but don't really tell a user what it is that you do exactly. Individual tweets, versus your bio, are where you can really benefit from content creativity.

Use a background image to personalize your Twitter

home page: Not only can an image help with branding, it's also an opportunity to provide some additional textual information (noting that this can't be linked or copy/pasted) on your home page. However, within your personalized background you can share important organization information, such as your tagline, which may not fit within your Twitter bio.

Listen: Use Twitter search engines for keyword searches around your brand. Tools like Summize/Twitter Search and TweetScan are good for this.

Post regularly (but not too regularly): Even if you need to have a couple of different people contributing content from time to time, it's important that you post regularly. That said, try not to drown out the conversation—keep your tweets to a maximum of five or ten per day (unless you are responding to questions that all your followers may be interested in). On the topic of responding, the more you engage in conversation the more successful your social media efforts. Also be careful how you manage multiple people with access to the same account (look back to chapter 5 for more tips on comanaging accounts).

Ask questions and solicit feedback from followers: Your customers can provide useful information if you pay attention to them. Twitter is great for getting opinions.

Provide value to your followers: Don't just push ads and brand messaging at them 24-7. Although you are online to promote your brand, try to include giving helpful tips for activities related to your product and discount offers, but try to avoid press releases. In chapter 5 I mentioned that @BlackBerryHelp is on

Twitter. When my new BlackBerry crashed after just a few weeks, I complained about the technology on Twitter and within two hours someone from @BlackBerryHelp responded to my tweet and sent me all the information I needed to get my device back up and running. In other words, your followers may drop you quickly if they think you're just doing your own PR and not creating any content.

Let people know you're on Twitter: Include a link to your Twitter account on your home page and in relevant e-mail signatures.

Never tweet anything you wouldn't want everyone to know: Twitter is a very public place where messages get handed around and can spread like wildfire, so be sure that you're comfortable sharing what you're saying. While this is not apparent when you sign up for Twitter, all of your public messages on the site are findable via Google and other search engines. In short, the messages are not private.

Talk about interesting things in your space: Direct talking about your product or business should be no more than half of your tweets, and don't feel that you need to discuss things very formally—again, this is about building relationships with real people, and people don't talk like press releases all the time.

Use links constructively: Whether they lead to your own content or to others' content, your tweets should give followers some indication of where the link will lead and why they might want to go there. There are tools like HootSuite that allow you to keep track of how many people clicked on the link you provided as well as what they are saying about you and what you tweet. There are many other third-party Twitter clients out there that you should keep in mind as well. Apps like TweetDeck and twhirl can make tweeting and keeping track of the conversation much easier.

Use direct messages when appropriate: If there is no value to other people's hearing your tweet, make it a direct message, especially when it's really a conversation between two people, but don't expect an immediate response. People are very busy and DM'ing shouldn't be used as an alternative to e-mail. Keep it light.

Follow those who follow you: While this advice may not always hold for individuals, it is hard to see the downside of this for companies. Following more people often exposes you to more people who will follow you back, thus creating a larger network to reach more people. They will be able to reach you more easily with direct messages, or just because the fact that you followed them means that you are listening to them.

Look up and follow companies and individuals with whom you already have relationships that are on Twitter and get involved in the conversation (where you can provide value).

It's best to use a desktop client such as TweetDeck or Twitterfall in order to monitor and customize searches such as your business name. These tools also allow you to group the people you follow in order to clear out some of the noise created by what can, at first, be a rather overwhelming experience.

SOCIAL NETWORKING

Facebook

Banned from some offices, invaluable in others, Facebook is everywhere. This site is a social networking service where friends connect online. Although Facebook started as a student-only site, it is now a popular destination for people of all ages and for companies from around the world. Facebook allows you to post notes, photos, videos, events, and more to your friends. It is an excellent platform to build up a network of "fans" and promote a conversation. There are also some common Facebook terms you should know:

Wall: This is where friends leave comments, photos, links, and more. The wall is where the majority of conversation happens on Facebook.

Status Update: This is where users leave messages about what they're doing now.

Profile: This is what users see for your account information.

Friends: This is where you can see your list of friends and add friends.

Settings: This is where you can change your information, notifications, and more.

Fan Pages: This will allow you to have more than five thousand people in your network. Having a fan page also means that you do not have to accept each user on an individual basis, saving you the time and frustration of clicking everyone's invite.

Here are tips for making the most effective use of Facebook as a social media tool:

Friend other people: Search for people in your network and suggest they join your fan page.

Post regularly: When you post photos to Flickr, videos to YouTube, messages to Twitter, or posts to your blog, you should also cross-post this content or links to Facebook (there are many specialized applications that will help you to do this automatically).

Engage with your fans: Communicate back and forth with your fans via their walls. Provide value to your followers (don't just push ads and brand messaging at them). This could include helpful tips or upcoming activities related to your product.

Let people know you're on Facebook: Include a link to your Facebook account on your home page and in relevant e-mail signatures.

Never post anything you wouldn't want everyone to know: Facebook is a very public place where messages get handed around and can spread like wildfire, so be sure that you're comfortable sharing what you're saying.

Talk about interesting things in your area/space: Direct talking about your product or business should be no more than half of your updates, and don't feel that you need to discuss things formally—again, this is about building relationships with real people.

Use links constructively: Whether they lead to your own content or to others' content, your posts should give followers some indication of where the link will lead and why they might want to go there.

Start slowly and build: Remember that's it's better to work up to speed, increasing frequency, instead of starting with a lot of posts and dwindling over time. As mentioned above, install the Twitter application so that your Twitter status updates also update your Facebook account.

Use Facebook Connect: Facebook Connect is a very simple way of having people register on your Web site. Facebook Connect allows them to use their existing Facebook account to log in and post feedback on your site. Users have the option of sharing their feedback with all of their Facebook friends as well. This huge personal network is incredibly valuable, and Facebook Connect allows you to use that data and create social graphs of who your customers are and who their friends are. My video podcast, *commandN*, uses Facebook Connect to bring our community together. Since we've built the site using Wordpress, Facebook Connect becomes a very easy tool to plug into the page (again, just another advantage to using software such as Wordpress is that its community updates and improves on a regular basis).

MySpace

Like Facebook, MySpace is a social networking site where friends can connect and share messages and content. Although MySpace continues to serve millions of users, these days it tends not to be as popular a destination for social media efforts as Facebook. While Facebook's membership continues to grow, MySpace's traffic is declining. According to Compete.com numbers, My-Space's U.S. traffic was equal to Facebook's as recently as December 2008, but the site had 60 percent fewer unique visitors than Facebook by October 2009. However, MySpace tends to cater to a music-oriented audience, offering free song streaming on its member pages, which makes it a preferred destination for the music industry. In short, if you are a musician promoting your new album, then MySpace is absolutely the right place to focus your social media efforts.

Flickr

Flickr is one of the most popular photo-sharing sites on the Web. As of June 2009, the Yahoo-owned service claims to host more than 3.6 billion images. Aside from acting as a home to billions of pictures, Flickr is an active online community of users. The site recently redesigned its search functionality, making it one of the best places to find photos on the Web.

Flickr is a great place to host your photos for all your products or events, and pictures of your company officers for easy download to be used by the media and shared across other social media sites. It is an easy platform for you to take and upload photos from your mobile phone and now includes support for video. When taking pictures, professional photographer Chase Jarvis says it best: "The best camera is the one that's with you." In other words, don't be shy about using your iPhone, Black-Berry, or other mobile device to snap great shots to share online.

Ning

Ning.com lets you start your own social network and communicate with those who are most passionate about your product or ideas. It provides some of the same functionality as Facebook or MySpace. You can post videos and photos and comment on one another's walls. Each user can have a customized page of his or her own and can link and connect with others. The site has grown considerably since it first launched in October of 2005 and now boasts over a million Ning Networks. It is free to join, but if you wish to control or limit the number of ads shown on the site you can opt to pay a monthly fee.

VIDEOS

We're living in an age of video, so for most organizations online video production should be a component of your marketing plan. In fact, we're almost at a point now where if you can't see it on the Web it just didn't happen. And today, anyone can be a producer, director, cameraman, or host. Sometimes the same person plays all four roles at once. Video is no longer the exclusive medium of large, well-funded studios or production companies. The tools for recording our lives have become so ubiquitous that it really isn't a question of whether or not your marketing should include video, but how. While potentially the most expensive of the social media tools, it also has the most potential to make an impact. Many companies are choosing, at minimum, to feature a well-produced "About Us" video on their home page. If you don't think that a video from your business makes sense, take a look at many of the leading organizations in your space and monitor over the next few months how some of them are taking the video leap. On the Web, the more creative you are the better chance you have to be seen. For example, during the holiday season of 2009, an iPhone app maker that launched a fun little download called Unicorn Me, which allowed users to place unicorn horns and scenes behind their favorite photos, posted a video depicting the app "in real life." The company's team hit the streets with a cardboard cut-out replicating what the app does digitally, serving up some entertaining video of pedestrians standing on sidewalks smiling in a pair of unicorn horns.

You may find yourself at any video kiosk of any of the big-box stores staring at the seemingly endless number of equipment choices available to you and wondering, "What is all this stuff for?" Well, I'm here to help you understand all the resources you have at your disposal. So how do you shoot something that is watchable? First, you need the right tools.

Camera

If you are a video production novice, there's no need to complicate your life with an expensive high definition (HD) camera that shoots large video files when lower-resolution footage will do just fine. It's better to keep your content files small and easy to stream and download.

HD and SD really only refer to the size of the image created, which is usually described in pixels, the tiny dots that make up a digital image on your computer screen. Anything larger than 720×480 pixels is generally considered HD; anything smaller is SD. The real secret is not what you shoot on but how you shoot it. Real quality comes from having decent audio, solid shooting techniques, and proper lighting, HD or not.

Whether you choose HD or SD, you need to make sure that the camera has some way to attach an external microphone to it. Many online video creators are opting for the Flip video camera, which is a point-and-shoot style of camera that makes recording as easy as pushing a big red button. This user-friendly camera provides great ease of use, but there is no way to attach an external microphone and you won't get high-quality sound recording from the camera's built-in mic. If you want to produce high-quality video for a company feature you will need to spend a little more on equipment, including microphones. However, a Flip video camera will still do the trick for off-the-cuff moments in the office or at an event.

Microphones

A microphone is a critical component of any video initiative because audio quality is arguably more important than video quality (think about how much easier it is to watch a grainy video than it is to listen to scratchy audio). Good audio will also ensure that you get your message delivered with clarity. In the world of video, audio is king.

Microphones generally fall into one of three general categories based on how they gather sound, which is called their "throw." Shotgun mics are the sticklike microphones you see on the large shoulder-based camera systems used by news crews. They are great at catching natural sound from wherever the camera is pointed, but that's about it. Shotgun microphone systems are very expensive, and if your subjects are not directly in front of you or are too far away, you won't record good sound. Unless you need to shoot high-quality commercials or record a podcast from someplace loud like a NASCAR track, you're probably better off with a cardioid or omnidirectional microphone. Both are handheld or lapel-attachable mics. Cardioid mics pick up sound from directly in front of the microphone, while omnidirectional mics, the most common type of microphone, pick up sound from all directions.

You will also have to choose between wireless and wired microphones. There are pros and cons to both. A wireless system can be more expensive, but it gives you and your subject more freedom to move around. The downside is that you could have interference from radio signals in the area and that could result in hisses or pops and cracks in your audio. With a hardwired system, the microphone cord is directly attached to the camera. What you lose in mobility you gain in solid, clear, easy-to-understand audio. The prices of small wireless systems continue to come down and the hardwired microphones are very affordable, so if possible, it's always better to have both kinds available, just in case.

I can't emphasize this enough: good sound is key to having a professional "look." You can invest in the best camera in the world, but if you can't hear the person speak it will "look" horrible.

Tripod

A steady image is a great image. A tripod is essential to your video-production kit; by keeping the camera steady, it provides a more professional look and a more watchable video (as well as adding to compression benefits, which we'll discuss later in this chapter). Your video tripod should have a fluid head, meaning that the part of the tripod you rest the camera on can be moved smoothly in all directions to allow you to follow movement when shooting footage. There are a number of other factors to consider, such as portability, weight, and adjustability, so head to the store and see what you can find within your budget that meets your needs. However, if you don't have the resources to purchase a tripod, there are a couple of tricks to keep your footage steady while shooting on your feet:

Zoom with your feet, not your lens. The more you zoom in using the controls on your camera the shakier the image will be. If you walk up to your subject and widen out your focal length you can achieve a much steadier look.

Find something to rest your camera on. You'd be surprised how a few books on a desk can turn into a tripod very quickly. In a pinch you can repurpose your still camera tripod, but it will lack the fluid head of a video tripod that allows you to do smooth pans (left to right) and tilts (up and down). Still, with a little creative flair and a gentle touch you can achieve great results on the fly.

Bounce Boards, Lights, and Studio Time

Expensive light kits are not necessary to shoot good videos. A lot of people feel that they need to have a studio to have a video show, but it's easy to improvise. The first show we did for my podcast *commandN* was shot on my computer's built-in camera, often next to a wall of colorful graffiti. Don't be afraid to think outside the box and get creative—head out to where you do your business, set up, and shoot. Location shooting has some difficulties associated with it, but it will add a sense of authenticity and transparency to your effort. Better yet, shoot your videos within your own corporate environment to share your company's culture (Blendtec, which I mentioned in chapter 4, did exactly this).

If you decide to shoot outside, a small, inexpensive bounce board (a board for reflecting light) and a few extra hands can make all the difference in the world. These reflectors or bounce boards are available at all photo and video stores and usually come with one white side and one silver or gold side. The idea here is to bounce the light back into the frame of your shot in order to get rid of any shadows that may have been created by the position of the sun or any lights that are indoors and close to where you are shooting.

Getting out is the best way to spice up your look and create something different. It's also the quickest way to make the task fun and something people want to be a part of . . . even in the winter!

When you head outside, keep your light in mind: where is it, what kind of light is it, and how long will you have it? Overcast light is very soft and nice, so if you think that you need to wait until the sun comes out, think again. The clouds act as a giant softbox; they make the light appear softer and tend to saturate colors more. If you are outside during the middle hours of the day, try to avoid the noontime sun. It can be harsh and create unwanted shadows under the eyes as well as washing out colors. Sunsets are great, as are mornings, so try to schedule shoots around those times. You'll be happy you did.

Shooting Tips

Before you walk through the door, have a plan.

All stories have a beginning, middle, and end, so when you go out to shoot you should have a clear idea of where you are going. You certainly don't need a massive script. Do create a rough script, but don't feel obliged to follow every detail of it. Always leave lots of room for spontaneity and creativity and be assured . . . if something can go wrong, it probably will.

There have been volumes written about how to make good videos, but there are a few rules you can use right off the bat that will get you in the game quickly while avoiding some common mistakes.

Rule of thirds: Imagine your image is divided up into a three-by-three square grid. Try to avoid putting your main subject in the middle of this square. Place the person's head off to either the left or the right side and have their nose and eyes pointing to the empty space. This extra space is called speaking room. The host is allowed to look directly into the lens for the most part because he or she is giving information directly to the viewer and guiding the story along.

Vary the shots in an interview: During questions, try to reposition the shot slightly for each answer. A little closer here, or a different angle there, can make a huge difference when it comes time to edit the video, making the final piece more interesting to watch. However, be careful not to have the camera angle too low below the "eye-line" (the imaginary line from the eye of your subject to the lens). It should stay around horizontal. If you dip too low you end up shooting up the nose, and if you are too high you'll end up looking down on your subject.

Avoid having a zoom as part of your shot: Try to reposition the composition of your shot in between answers, not during them. That slow zoom-in that you see on *60 Minutes* as the sweat begins to bead on the interviewee's forehead was shot by a professional. If you make an error the effect is lost and you have one very distracting piece of video footage.

Shoot B-roll: *B-roll* is the industry term for images that are not part of the interview. If you are shooting an interview with your CEO about your new widget plant, take some time to shoot the plant itself: the exterior of the building, the internal workings of the plant at each stage, and shots of the employees who make it all come together. This way the story of the birth of the widget can be seen while the CEO talks, making for a much more watchable video. This doesn't just apply to widget factories, though. Wherever you are, shoot a little bit of the space around you, faces of people, or details of the room or area you are in. This can prove more than useful in the editing stages, especially when covering up voice-overs or narration.

Edit Etiquette

Most computers have video editing software built in or available for a free download. You won't need to run out and buy Final Cut Pro or Avid systems right away; iMovie for Macs and Windows Movie Maker for PCs offer very easy drag-and-drop interfaces for you to start out on. I won't detail the specific pros and cons of all the systems out there or their particular workflows, but here are some tips to making your videos watchable.

Capture and note-taking: Once you have your video ingested (which is just a fancy word that means transferred over) into the computer, either by FireWire or disc, sit down in front of the screen and review your footage. Take notes and be aware of what you absolutely must have to tell the story (this is called a paper edit).

Ignore most bells and whistles: There is no limit to what you can do to your video files with your editor. You can speed up, slow down, use transitions that look like book pages turning, and change the whole color of your video to look like it was shot back in the heyday of silent films. However, just because they are there doesn't mean you need to figure out a way to incorporate them. Almost all of your editing should be done with just a few basic techniques.

The cut: This is the most basic of all video edits. One shot stops and immediately the next one begins. Nearly all of your transitions should be cuts.

Fades: With fade-in, the screen starts black and your shot slowly appears. The opposite occurs for a fade-out. These are often employed at the start and end of a scene. They can also be used as a representation of the passage of time or an audio edit of an interview where there was no B-roll available as a cutaway.

Titles and keys: Titles (text on the screen) can be great for conveying locations or other useful information without a long voice-over. On-screen graphics, often called keys or lower-thirds (for example, a Web site address), will help identify who is speaking without direct introduction and should match titles or any graphical opening sequence to keep brand continuity.

Insert editing: This is a technique that involves splicing a cutaway shot into a long master shot. You can use this to clean up the audio from the master shot. For example, while the CEO is explaining how widgets are made and where they are used, you can cut out any coughs or long pauses by inserting cutaway shots of B-roll in between.

Encoding and Streaming

Next up is the all-important step of encoding your video for release onto one of the many video hosting sites online. Encoding is the process of converting your video from the format you shot and edited it in to a format that is compatible with your online hosting service. Your video editing software has options for encoding, and you should follow the specifications of your video hosting site when exporting your file into the correct format.

Once your video is encoded, it's time to put it online. As with podcasts, you can use hosting services, but by far the most common way to deliver video online is streaming.

There are many video hosting services that tend to aggregate separate audiences. For example, budding young webisode (online Web series) creators tend to choose Blip.tv for their episodic content, whereas film-school types and hardcore camera buffs choose Vimeo for its community of filmmakers and animation artists, but when it comes to online video you can't ignore the elephant in the room . . . YouTube!

YouTube is the number-one video-sharing site online. Launched in 2005, the service allows users to upload and embed videos. You now also have the ability to upload high-definition video to the YouTube player. The site is free to use. With a registered account, you have the option to approve comments.

With its billion video views per day, YouTube is, quite frankly, where the people are. It's the second most widely used search engine next to Google. The reach is incredible and provides a simple way to embed content onto almost every blogging platform that is widely used. Also, as a point of entry for the novice consumer or the producer, it is pretty straightforward to get up and running.

Be part of the community, build friends, and subscribe to other people's videos. Comment nicely and as often as you can. This is how community is built around your videos.

Tag your content with keywords. Tag again. Tag properly. Think of every word you can to describe your content and your ideas, so the search engine will see the video and post it on the side as "Related Video" or place it higher up in the search rankings. Treat your YouTube page the same way you would a blog, and post on a regular basis. But never post any videos you wouldn't want everyone to see: YouTube is a very public place where your video links get handed around.

Let people know you're on YouTube: include a link to your YouTube account on your home page and encourage your friends and fellow employees to subscribe to the account and offer honest feedback in the comments.

Video can be as simple or as elaborate as you can afford. One of the benefits of experimenting with video is that it's a medium that is easily shared online.

PODCASTS

Podcasting is a term that has caught our imaginations. Most radio shows are now podcasts, which just means that they are available as some form of digital download, most likely through iTunes but also in the form of direct downloads from the host Web site or other aggregators. The ease of posting and downloading podcasts translates into small but incredibly loyal audiences. Podcasting is a way to connect directly with your customers, your peers, and even your own employees.

Content

Podcasts are great for finding a very niche audience (for example, if you run a mom-and-pop coffee shop, a podcast about java beans, recipes, etc. might be a good fit). Since podcasts generally run between twenty and sixty minutes, you are really speaking to those who have decided to seek you out and are interested in what you have to say. This is where you can use your industry-specific jargon and your insight to talk to those who share your passion and zest for your chosen topic. If well done, a podcast can be the bedrock of your social media strategy, opening up the communication pathways to your most loyal customers or clients. In this area, niche is best—the more focused your podcast theme is, the higher its chance of success among your peers.

A computer will obviously be necessary to edit your final product and provide digital files for download, and you can use a digital voice recorder to gather interviews locally. With USB-powered microphones or headsets, you can conduct interviews remotely over Internet phone services like Skype or Vonage, recording the interview directly onto your computer using Audio Hijack Pro (which I use on my Mac) or other recording tools available on the market.

It is best to avoid your computer's built-in microphone or Web cam entirely since it will pick up too much ambient noise and make the podcast sound muddled. Nothing turns listeners away quicker than not being able to hear clearly what's being discussed. Keep this in mind when determining where to record your podcast. You'll want to find a small room that is relatively silent. Make sure that environmental noises won't interfere with your recording. Turning off air conditioners, fans, phones/faxes, and other noise-making devices is a good first step. You can also mitigate unwanted sound by recording at times when noise levels are at a minimum.

You may find that there is an echo in your podcast. This is a common occurrence and is caused by sound bouncing off of flat walls. Sometimes just placing foam or cloth in corners and along hard walls can help with this, but even just recording in a room with soft surfaces, like couches and carpets, can lessen the bounce. Once you have your setup ready to go, make sure that you as the host or anyone else who is helping with the recording of the show is wearing headphones and listening closely. If no one is monitoring the audio, you won't find out until after the interview if a mic was unplugged or background noise was interfering with your recording. The monitor should also determine the proper sound levels and listen for any distortion or excessive mouth noises such as lip-smacking or loud swallowing. If you're planning to use background music, don't have it playing while you record—this should be added to your track at the editing stage instead.

Apple computers have a wonderful sound editor called GarageBand that has a podcasting preset built into it, but there are also other free tools like Audacity that will make creating a podcast very simple.

Enhanced podcasts can be created on Macs and they can be viewed on any machine. They allow the ability to embed photos and links to content within the podcast. While not necessary, this can be a nice addition to your content.

Sample Show Timeline

Podcasts are also called "shows," whether they are audio or video. The best shows, whether they're on TV, on radio, or online, adhere to a specific format. The more you can stick to a format, the more your audience will become comfortable with that format and be comfortable with your show. A show timeline is simply a rundown of the content within your program. This is something that can be created very easily before each episode to keep the content (and conversation) on track. The format for a timeline can differ, depending on the full length of your show, but most will have some type of tease (promo) at the beginning, some music, an introduction, a few topics discussed, a summary, and some music to end off the show. Below is a sample timeline, which will give you an idea of what to include when planning your podcast.

- Show tease (who you are, what you're going to talk about): 30 seconds
- Intro music jingle (repeat for each show so listeners identify the jingle with your show): 10 seconds
- Topic 1: 3 minutes
- Stinger (a small sound or section of your intro music, used to separate your topics): 3 seconds
- Topic 2: 3 minutes
- Stinger: 3 seconds

- Topic 3: 3 minutes
- Stinger: 3 seconds
- Topic 4: 3 minutes
- Closing remarks (thank audience for listening, thank guests, talk about the next show briefly): 2 minutes
- Closing music jingle (suggest same as Intro music jingle): 30 seconds

Hosting Home

Web hosting, not to be confused with on-air talent, is the term used to describe where you store your podcast on the Web. There are a lot of free and inexpensive hosting sites like Libsyn or Hipcast that will host your podcast and also provide valuable statistics, such as how many people downloaded your show. They will also help you figure out how to list your show in iTunes, which is the number one place users go to get subscription-based audio and video content online.

Podcast Evaluation

Once you're up and running you can then evaluate your podcast using a variety of tools. If you are using a hosting service, they should be able to tell you how many times your show has been downloaded. If that number continues to increase, chances are you're providing some sort of value for your listeners and they are spreading the word. The next metric to measure would be an increase in your Web site traffic. As more people listen to the podcast they will probably visit your site. What feedback have you received? Make sure there is room for feedback on your Web site where you promote your podcast. For example, post each episode on your company's blog and enable comments so viewers or listeners can let you know what they think. Another great way to encourage feedback is to use a commenting tool such as Facebook Connect, which will allow anyone leaving a comment on your site to log in via his or her Facebook account. Finally, it does make sense on a regular basis to create an online survey to get more information about your podcast audience. One of the most useful and inexpensive survey tools on the Web is SurveyMonkey. Remember, if you ask your audience to spend time filling out a survey it's a good friending practice to offer them something in return (such as a chance to win a prize) and to make sure you keep your questions short and sweet.

Like experimenting with video online, your video podcast can be done very inexpensively if that's all you can budget. With an audio show, you can get up and running for less than $100 (along with a computer) and still have professional quality and gain a loyal audience following.

MOBILE TOOLS

One of the editors of *Harper's Magazine*, Bill Wasik, created the first flash mobs in Manhattan in the spring of 2003. Using text messaging and e-mails, he anonymously coordinated gatherings of strangers at specific locations and times to complete a specific action. One of these was to collectively shop for a rug in a Manhattan department store. Another involved about two hundred people clapping in unison for fifteen seconds in the lobby of the Hyatt. This ability to organize and execute, as a group, a particular action just by the power of mobile tech is astonishing.

According to Nielsen Mobile, more people now send text messages than do voicemail. Right now we have connections with everyone we know in our pockets, and the ability to build community immediately based on location-based mobile services is truly game-changing. In chapter 4, I described mobile apps, QR codes, SMS messages, and ring tones, which will all require an external team for execution. However, there is one way to leverage cutting-edge mobile technology in-house with free tools. Go live with the video camera inside your mobile device whenever you can and tell people about it. Reverse the flash mob model and bring the crowd to you, virtually.

Some of the live tools that exist online include Ustream and Stickam. Although services have a number of different features, the goal of each is to allow you to broadcast content live online. When Margaret Atwood hosted a live book launch party from her home, she used Ustream. The live element can be great for companies looking to stream events or host organized Web conversations. For example, if you run a small organic food store you might consider hosting a short monthly live Web show to teach audiences online about the benefits of eating organic. The majority of these services are free, making it a cost-effective way to build an audience. Also, many of these services offer up mobile apps so you can in fact stream live from your telephone. However, for the best quality, you are better off to do a live show in front of a laptop.

If you're using your computer you will need to have a fast system with a camera and microphone attached. If you are on your phone you'll need a compatible handset and a 3G or higher connection. (All of the sites out there that provide these services have a minimum requirements page that you may consult.) Make sure you have the proper equipment. If you have the money, spend it. A good start would be an external microphone, a Web cam or camcorder with mediocre to great video quality, and most important, a computer that can run the software required to stream.

You'll also need to create a show page on whatever live streaming site you choose. When you set up your account, you'll have the option of simultaneously posting your video to Twitter and Facebook via the site.

Now it's time to go live. This is digital public speaking. If you are uncomfortable with the idea of being in front of large groups of strangers, then maybe this isn't the best choice for you.

Be relevant to your core theme; don't start to live stream at a baseball game or the county fair if you are in financial management or the reinsurance game. Live streaming can be a great way to reach out to your audience, provided that it is somewhere that is consistent with your other endeavors. If you are a baseball bat manufacturer, then by all means stream the Little League game, or if you're a pharmaceutical sales rep stream the workshop you're giving, but try not to deviate too far from your content path. Again, mobile applications are opening up a world where any organization can "go live" at any time, giving audiences a real-time real-life experience.

WIKIS

A wiki is fairly easy to set up. If you know how to do simple word processing, the majority of wikis operate in the same way. The most popular wiki in the world is Wikipedia, which launched using free software called MediaWiki software. For a wide variety of organizations, MediaWiki is a good option to kick off a wiki. When working to establish a successful wiki, whether it's for internal or external use, have someone on your team be responsible for "owning" the wiki content, which will need updating on a regular basis. With at least one person spearheading your wiki efforts, that individual can ensure that your organization is using its wiki to its full potential. Like Wikipedia, a wiki needs constant attention and contributions.

LISTENING

If you put a commercial on television, you're going to have a difficult time figuring out exactly what viewers thought when they saw it. In the Web world, the art of listening is definitely something to learn. Without having to do expensive research or conduct lengthy surveys, you have a wealth of information about what people think of your brand at your fingertips. Even if you're strapped for cash and time, you can easily gather all the information you need—you just have to figure out how to find it. There are a range of tools to monitor your image online, from a simple Google search to paid reputation management services. For most companies, the top three listening tools on this list may be all you need, and they're all free and easy to use. As you start to want to gather more specific information about your online image, traffic, and campaigns, check out some of these other tools to beef up your listening power. These listening tools will also help you to answer four specific questions that are key to social media listening.

THE FOUR W'S OF SOCIAL MEDIA LISTENING

1. **Who:** determine who is talking about your brand; this will include people who might be identified as brand evangelists.
2. **What:** determine what is the general message out there about your brand, including both negative and positive feedback.
3. **Where:** determine where most of the conversation is happening, which will help you to determine where you should be.
4. **When:** determine the time and dates of conversations, which will help you to determine if you ran a successful campaign or should be more active during these times.

Google Alerts

Google Alerts is a free service that provides the user with e-mail updates of current, relevant Google search results based on keywords the user selects. It also allows you to subscribe to updates via an RSS feed. The alerts track everything from blog posts to traditional and emerging media news articles, videos, groups, and so on. One especially handy feature is the ability to monitor developing news stories—perhaps about your product or brand. For example, I have set up a Google Alert to keep me updated about when people are talking about *Power Friending* online. If you're only going to use one listening tool, Google Alerts is your best bet.

Summize

Summize, which was recently purchased by Twitter, is a Web tool that allows the user to access the latest and most relevant product reviews and sentiments on thousands upon thousands of products like movies, books, and appliances. Summize visually collects and summarizes the best and worst reviews—while still portraying accurate average perceptions of the product—so that the user does not have to read through hundreds of comments to find an answer. It's a great way for consumers to make purchases they feel confident in and it allows companies to review how consumers feel about their products and brands.

Technorati

In addition to Technorati being the world's sixth largest social media property, it also serves as an extremely useful tool for companies and consumers alike to access what people worldwide are saying about products, brands, and services on millions of blogs and over 1.5 million new blog posts daily. It does this via vertical content channels and tag filtering. Technorati is known for surfacing the best online global conversations because it tracks the authority, influence, and popularity of blogs on top of providing content searches. Add this to its top-notch indexing—which includes trend tracking and the ability to create custom microchannels—and you've got the leading tool in finding the most popular and influential conversations about your product or brand.

TweetBeep

TweetBeep is Twitter's version of Google Alerts, and is especially useful considering the fact that a great deal of consumer-generated discussion occurs on Twitter. The service allows you to receive alerts whenever someone mentions you or your brand in the Twitter world. It's great because it refreshes and sends you updates hourly. What is especially helpful is that it tracks any URLs posted about you or linking to you—even if they've been shortened (like bit.ly or tinyurl.com, or other URL shorteners).

Visible Technologies

Visible Technologies has a few advantages, as it offers two online brand monitoring services. The first is truCAST—a comprehensive solution for social media analysis and participation used by companies that are keen on engaging with social media communities. The service allows the user to play a participatory role in the process of consumer dialogue. A neat feature here is that it allows you to comment on blogs and forums mentioning you or the brand directly from the application platform. The second service is TruView, which protects and promotes your brand's reputation online and allows you to take ownership of your brand's Google results by ensuring that there is positive and up-to-date information at the top of the search engine when a user searches your company. When used together, these tools can be very effective at controlling and surveying your brand online while participating in the process.

Sentiment Metrics

Sentiment Metrics provides a reputation management service tool that, like the others to follow, keeps you informed on what is being said about you, your product, or your brand. It monitors this information on blogs, news media sites, and forums. The difference here is that it tracks the sentiment as well and lets you know whether the conversation taking place about your brand is positive, negative, or neutral.

Trackur

Trackur provides users with monitoring plans from $18 per month to $197 per month that track the keywords you insert and organize the results in a dashboard application. The frequency and size of updates depend on the package. Trackur was built by Andy Beal, a leading expert in reputation management, which definitely adds credibility to this Web service. Trackur is also one of the only reputation management services that allows the user or a company to take the dashboard for a test drive, free of charge and no credit card required, to see if the product works for them before purchasing.

BrandsEye

BrandsEye offers users several reputation managing packages from $1 per month to $350 per month. The application tracks every online mention of the user's brand and produces a score that reflects your current reputation online over time. A good feature this tool offers is the ability to tag mentions of your brand and rank them according to a number of different criteria. The only downside to this product is that the more you plan to use it, the more it costs.

BuzzLogic

BuzzLogic is the home of the BuzzLogic Insights application where you can find, communicate with, and compare influencers in your industry. The application provides you with a collaborative dashboard, which lets you know which bloggers are talking about you. The neat part about this collaborative dashboard is that you are able to share this information within your company like a wiki. The application also allows you to create "Watch Lists" where you can track specific bloggers, blogger profile lists, and social maps—to see who links to whom. Buzz-Logic Insights caters mainly to the needs of two major groups—

marketers and PR people. The marketing benefits include gaining product feedback, understanding brand reputation, and receiving specialized monthly readership statistics. The PR benefits include the ability to build relationships with influential bloggers, discover new influencers, and track products and content that matter to them.

Techrigy

Techrigy, founded in 2006, has been referred to by TechCrunch as "Google on steroids." It provides an enormous fleet of features, including an exceptional one that allows you not only to view trending graphs over time, but to isolate specific dates and geo-locations. Other great tools include conversation-tracking ability and sentiment reviews (positive and negative).

Radian6

Radian6, which is one of the more popular tracking tools, provides users with a dashboard where they are able to insert keywords and monitor them in one place. After a user inserts the keywords, Radian6 automatically tracks their use—in real time—on blogs, image-sharing sites like Flickr, microblogging sites like Twitter, and so on. After tracking, the dashboard generates a report and analysis of the results. A cool feature Radian6 offers is that it tracks how viral any particular keyword is by monitoring conversational dynamics.

Cision

Cision (powered by Radian6) is the home of Cision Social Media, a service that monitors over 100 million blogs, tens of thousands of online forums, and over 450 leading rich media sites. Cision has been tracking and monitoring traditional media sites for decades, so they can integrate those findings into their emerging media data, building one overarching solution. Cision is also unique because it offers 24/7 coverage.

TNS Cymfony

TNS Cymfony offers the Orchestra Platform, which works on a National Language Processing engine that automatically identifies, classifies, and tracks blogs, traditional and emerging media sites, and any online space that mentions you or your brand. What sets this platform apart from others is that it analyzes what is being said about you and by whom, not just where to find it. The service dissects articles down to paragraphs and sentences, to determine if your mention is brief or if it is the focus of what is being discussed. It also analyzes how the various mentions relate to one another.

BuzzMetrics

BuzzMetrics is a service that acts like a doctor for your brand's reputation. It supplies the user with key brand health metrics and consumer commentary from all user/consumer-generated media sites. In addition, the service provides the user with a brand health scorecard to compare with the competition. A unique aspect of this product is that it contains a ThreatTracker, which lets you know—in real time—of any negative comments about your brand so you can stay on top of fixing the problem and diminish any potential flare-ups of controversy.

BuzzMetrics is provided by Nielsen, a well-known leader in the brand awareness and marketing fields. And one of the leaders of user-generated media, Pete Blackshaw, is actively behind this unique service.

SHARING AND MEASURING

In terms of collecting and sharing useful links, images, and discussions on the Web, the following content-sharing tools become extremely helpful. Many of these tools are used inside an organization to facilitate collaboration when working on a project. For a social media manager monitoring a brand online, these tools are exceptionally useful for two things.

1. Staying on top of social media news, case studies, and more.
2. Tracking and quickly bookmarking links that you want to remember and use as part of your regular social media reports inside your organization (Delicious is particularly useful for this, so you can simply bookmark a link and move on, knowing that it will always be saved on the Web).

Google Reader and Delicious

An effective but often overlooked combination of tools is Google Reader and Delicious. Google Reader serves as a simple, personalized feed reader where users can organize their feeds and rank and share them with their networks. In conjunction with this tool, Delicious is a great tool for creating a portable bookmark collection with links to everything about your brand. The nice thing with Delicious is that the site lets you share your feed with everyone in your network.

Google Reader aggregates all the updates from your favorite blogs and news sites into a single feed that you can read like email. You have the option of flagging your favorite items and sharing them with other members of your network.

Delicious changes the way you save bookmarks. In your web browser, you have the option of nesting your favorite sites in a series of folders. With Delicious you use tags, specific key words to categorize content, to keep your sites organized. For example, I may save an article from a website about declining sales of newspapers. I may tag this item with many keywords, including journalism, ad sales, market decline, web growth, and paper industry. All these items could have been mentioned in the article, and I may wish to refer to that information at a later time. If I enter any one of these terms into the search box on Delicious, this article along with any others that I have tagged with, say, "journalism" will appear as well.

By sharing accounts on Google Reader and Delicious, users

can create a database with a team or the entire organization. Designs or innovative strategies can be shared within the group, and you can keep tabs on your own brand and those of your competitors.

Google Analytics

In terms of analytical and statistical data, Google Analytics is exceptional. It helps you analyze your company's blog traffic, subscriber count, keyword optimization, and other trends. It provides insight into marketing effectiveness and offers many solutions to any potential problem areas it may stumble upon during its research. One great feature is the service's click-by-click tool that shows you exactly how users navigate through the site.

Woopra

A very interesting tool called Woopra is also starting to make some noise in the analytics world, thanks to its real-time Web statistics, which definitely has that "wow" factor when you're trying to accurately and regularly monitor your site's traffic. This tool offers a free version, but most companies will need to invest in the paid version because of traffic demands.

Google Trends

Google allows you to compare up to five different topics and then displays the frequency with which those terms have been searched and graphs them for you based on timelines extending up to five years in the past. They also show what Google News stories those keywords have appeared in and where geographically most of the searches have appeared. When we punched the name of our podcast, *commandN*, into Google Trends, we found out that the second biggest region where searches for our podcast occurred was in Australia. We knew from the comments that a lot of people from down under enjoyed the show, but this helped to focus our efforts at reaching out to our commonwealth cousins and is always in the back of our heads when discussing any future initiatives with our audience.

Facebook Lexicon

Facebook offers a similar feature called Lexicon that scans all Facebook wall posts (the space on each user's page where their friends can post public messages) for up to five words as well as two word phrases. Walls on Facebook are a great resource to spread information. Unlike Google, which aggregates searches from all over the planet, the information spread on Facebook is from friend to friend, a much more reliable and trustworthy source of endorsements.

———

Some organizations I've worked with have the most trouble with execution. Whether it's a lack of ideas or too many ideas, this stage of their social media strategy often falls short if they don't return to (and follow) the rules discussed at the beginning of this book: authenticity, bravery, and consistency. When these rules are followed, when the project has a community manager at the helm, and when the right tools are used to track and measure success, engagement follows. However, there are some companies that forget all of these key factors, proceeding quickly down the path to failure. Both successes and failures in the social media space provide some excellent learning tips and tools. The next two chapters will discuss popular examples of organizations that power friended well, and infamous examples of those that did not.

Chapter seven

The Failures

Early in the fall of 2006, Laura and Jim started to document their journey across America, parking their RV for free in Walmart lots from Las Vegas to Georgia. They took photos of Walmart employees they met and gushed about their experiences visiting the giant retailer. And Walmart went along for the ride, literally. Many readers believed that the couple used their own money for the trip, and that Laura and Jim shared stories of big-box love out of the goodness of their hearts. Quite quickly, however, bloggers started to get suspicious about all of the glowing reviews on the site. Then *BusinessWeek* uncovered the real story behind the couple.

It turned out that the Edelman PR agency worked with Walmart to set up the entire campaign. Although there were some elements of truth throughout the short life of the blog, what was missing goes back to the first rule of Internet friending: authenticity. Walmart did not openly explain anywhere on the blog that they paid for the couple's RV and travel expenses, and also paid them for each written entry on the site. When word came out that Walmart was involved to this extent, bloggers attacked the "fake" blog. The negative reaction forced the retailer to take "Wal-Marting Across America" offline. Years later, conversations about the fumble still live on in the social media marketing world.

If you make a mistake online, your company's reputation can take an irreparable hit if you don't manage the situation well. A friend of mine has a T-shirt that says, "WHAT HAPPENS IN VEGAS, STAYS ON TWITTER, YOUTUBE, AND FLICKR." It's true: there is nowhere to hide from your past in today's world of social media. However, you can avoid potential fumbles by learning from the missteps of some other companies that have made some long-lasting mistakes. Many of these #fail stories could have been avoided if these companies followed the ABCs of friending and stuck to a long-term strategic social media plan.

SKITTLES' TWITTER CAMPAIGN

In early March 2009, the candy brand Skittles relaunched its product by giving its Web site (Skittles.com) a social media makeover. In an attempt to reach out to a younger demographic, the new home page featured a real-time Twitter feed displaying all tweets containing the word "Skittles." Sounds like a pretty innovative idea, but think about what a "free-for-all feed" really means. If someone decided to mention Skittles on Twitter and tuck some profanity into their 140 characters or less, then Skittles was promoting these messages loud and proud on its home page. Such an open campaign did not give Skittles the family-friendly image it wanted. With zero guidance, users began slamming the brand and its new marketing strategy, a lot of times just to watch their negative notes appear on the Mars-owned company's home page. For example, Mike Butcher wrote, "Skittles give you cancer and is the cause of all world evil." Hundreds more people included profanity in their tweets, making some visitors think that the Skittles home page must have been hacked. This wave of uncensored messages was, obviously, not the desired effect.

Regardless of the fact that there were a slew of tweets streaming in, it quickly became apparent that Skittles took the wrong approach in what seemed like a rushed marketing maneuver. There are several reasons why they should have taken more time to thoughtfully develop their strategy. For one, Skittles did not enter the social media space in an authentic way. At the time, the company itself wasn't actively broadcasting on Twitter to connect with its customers. Moreover, this campaign didn't involve any actual interaction between Skittles and its customers. The ready-made feed was a fairly low-effort initiative but with larger-than-expected negative consequences.

The candy company quickly pulled the Twitter campaign, realizing that it didn't reflect well on the company's brand to have such unregulated content on its home page. Although we can't accuse Skittles of lacking the bravery to hand over control to the masses, or the ability to leverage new technology, it made a critical error that killed what could have been an excellent marketing campaign. If only Skittles had opened a door to a two-way conversation between brand and consumer, and encouraged a collective sense of community, the campaign would have likely yielded better results. For example, Skittles could have easily posted a select number of moderated Twitter comments to its home page with a catchy title such as "Today's Skittles Buzz." Skittles could have launched a Skittles contest for its Twitter fans, asking them to create a Skittles song for a chance to win a lifetime supply of Skittles. This failed campaign made such an impact in the online world that it is still a key discussion point on Skittles' Wikipedia page.

GENERAL MOTOR'S VIRAL MARKETING CAMPAIGN

In 2006, General Motors encouraged the general public to create their own video ads for the then-new Chevy Tahoe. Ample amounts of video and audio footage of the SUV were provided on the contest Web site, and users were told to get as creative as possible with the material in an attempt to create some user-generated viral videos. This type of campaign, asking users to create custom content, is fairly common in the social media world.

What seemed like a pretty innovative way to market a new automobile quickly backfired when environmentalists created dozens of negative ads scolding GM for lacking green-friendly products. For example, one YouTube ad called the "Chevy Tahoe Commercial Parody" told the story of how the new Chevy Tahoe ruined our environment. "We paved the prairies. We deforested the hills. We strip-mined our mountains. And sold ourselves for oil. To bring you this beautiful machine." This video has more than 100,000 views and dozens of comments. The criticisms were broad and included accusations of how GM is contributing to global warming, not protesting the war over oil in Iraq, and not making the roads safe for pedestrians and bikers. The ABC News program *Nightline* picked up on the campaign controversy in a segment called "Sign of the Times." The news reporter interviewed one of the anti-Tahoe ad creators who had this to say: "Why is an American company acting as a pusher to an addiction to Middle Eastern oil? This thing's a mini tank." Ouch.

The errors that GM made here are pretty vast. In a time when the automobile industry is often presented in a negative light, when global warming is at the forefront of many political agendas, a company might want to be more in touch with what a large segment of its customers really think of its products (and not wish to relinquish total control over their advertising). Perhaps if more general research had been done prior to releasing the ad, or if GM had made more of an effort to communicate with its critics after the negative ads began rolling in, much more brand damage could have been avoided, repaired, or even improved. Although there is a push across all social media campaigns to avoid too much moderation, it is critical to maintain some control over your brand online.

WALMART'S FACEBOOK CAMPAIGN

In 2007, Walmart made another major social media error when it launched a social media campaign utilizing the pages feature on Facebook to promote its "stylish" dorm room products. The campaign was called "Roommate Style Match." However, Walmart is not known for stylish products—its products are known for being *cheap*. A similar campaign by Target, with its youth-oriented, design-friendly aesthetic, met with great success. Walmart's attempt did not fare so well, as evidenced by the many derogatory comments like this one on its Facebook pages:

> Do people realize WHY prices are so low at Walmart? cause THEY DO NOT PAY LIVING WAGES to employees in America and THEIR CHINESE FACTORIES ARE BASICALLY SLAVERY. WAL-MART IS HATEFUL AND IS A BLIGHT ON AMERICA. Facebook should CUT ALL ITS TIES to Walmart. GET WALMART OFF FACEBOOK!

Walmart is a repeat offender; time and again they completely miss the point of social media. Any effort they make that focuses on talking *to* consumers will fail because social media is about talking *with* people and engaging in conversation. There is also a lesson to be learned here about knowing your role as a business, and how your consumers perceive you. Walmart should have focused on connecting with consumers and encouraged discussions based on functional products that every student needs, products that are cost-friendly—which is what the giant retailer is all about.

Although many companies such as GM and Walmart are not well liked among some influential groups of people, there is a great opportunity for them to use social media on the Web to find out, from customers, how they can improve their organizations. Of course no one likes to hear the negative comments, but to be successful in these new times it's a necessity. Being open to all sides of a conversation is in line with the second rule of Internet friending, bravery. Hiding behind social media profiles while the community bashes your brand doesn't help anyone.

BRINGPOPCORN.COM'S SPAMMING DIGG CAMPAIGN

In February of 2007, Alex Hunter, operator of the Web site Bringpopcorn.com, committed a big no-no in the collective community of the content-sharing site Digg. He reached out to ten top Diggers (the highest-ranked and most influential users of the site) and offered them each five hundred dollars if they would get his Web site listed on Digg's home page. (Digg users vote URL links up or down on the site depending on whether or not they like or recommend them. The content with the most positive votes moves up to the home page on Digg, where more people will see it.) This strategy throws all authenticity out the window. This is the message Hunter wrote:

> Hello,
>
> I need a favor. I run a website bringpopcorn.com.
>
> Would you get my website to the Digg first page, and if successful I'll pay $500.
>
> The site is of interest to most Digg users anyhow, it's just people only listen to top Digg users.
>
> If interested please email back.
>
> Alex

Not only does this go against the general concept and purpose of Digg, which is about letting people share content they like with like-minded online friends, but this type of solicitation and lazy marketing is exactly the type of ploy that will get you blacklisted—fast. Alex Hunter and his get-traffic-fast plan were quickly exposed and he was also reportedly banned from Netscape.com after he was discovered running twenty phony accounts which he used to shamelessly promote his site. This type of approach is often referred to as *spam*—something no one likes.

The moral of this story? Social media and its participants do not respond well to spam. If you believe your content is of value and that people will enjoy it, it is much better to promote it yourself in an authentic and transparent way rather than paying for others to do it for you on the sly. Also, if it is of interest to consumers, they will submit it to content-sharing sites in an open and honest way. I can't emphasize enough how sensitive the social media community is to scams like the one Hunter tried to pull off.

PIZZA HUT'S TWITTER CAMPAIGN

The pizza industry hasn't had an easy time with social media (remember poor Patrick Doyle and the Domino's You-Tube employee scandal?). In early 2009, Pizza Hut decided it wanted to get in on the social media frenzy. The company posted an ad for a young, hip intern—or a "twintern," as they called it—who would create and manage a Twitter account for the company. They were looking for someone who knew how to properly retweet and use hashtags and someone who "speaks fluent LOL" (a reference to the short-form tech language that is developing online). There were a couple of issues that erupted because of this recruitment campaign.

First off, when breaking into a community that millions of people around the world consider extremely valuable, it might be a good idea not to belittle them by making fun of the way they communicate via the service (e.g., the cutesy request for someone "who speaks fluent LOL"). Try market-testing your campaign ideas in front of the audience you're reaching out to before you go live (and do this on a consistent basis).

Second off, followers and general users couldn't quite wrap their heads around the idea that Pizza Hut wanted to hire an intern who knew nothing about the company prior to their hiring to handle the largest and most direct line it had between their business and their consumers (after all, there are tens of millions of Twitter users, an audience that might require someone with a little more experience). When attempting to boost your brand online, it makes sense to hire someone with some social media experience and some experience in your industry (in this case, the food business).

Li Evans from SearchMarketingGurus.com is also critical of Pizza Hut's intern hiring strategy. She writes, "Would any company be crazy enough to let an intern who doesn't know the inner workings of their global brand (carefully crafted messaging they've spent millions on) plan, prepare, run and speak at an international press event that launches your brand on an international stage?"

This story should not deter any business from heading to Twitter or other social media Web sites to recruit online (and it should not deter companies from hiring students, who often have more knowledge about social media than top-level executives). I found one of the best people I've ever worked with via an online search. What's great about recruiting online is that you can target specific networks of people, including those networks inside your organization. Sometimes, this can be a much better approach than heading to a recruitment agency. The only thing you need to be careful about is publicly advertising positions that are currently filled (in other words, if you plan to let someone go and hire someone else to replace them, you might want to be more discreet than publishing this post on the Web).

To be fair, Pizza Hut is currently active on Twitter and is now doing a great job of replying to customer concerns. They also actively promote the world hunger cause on their account, a socially conscious behavior that is appreciated online and offline. Their "twintern" does manage the account, but as it explains in the bio section, there are also others from the Pizza Hut Twitter team who are involved. Finally, Pizza Hut did get a ton of press, including a story in *The New York Times*, with this creative hiring approach.

MOLSON CANADIAN FACEBOOK PHOTO CONTEST CAMPAIGN

In 2007, Molson, which is one of the largest brewing companies in the world, launched a controversial social media campaign. It kicked off a contest called "The Molson Canadian Nation Campus Challenge" targeting college and university students aged nineteen to twenty-four years old (nineteen is the legal drinking age in most parts of Canada). The ad, which was posted on Molson's Facebook page, called for students to send in party photos from their campus and demonstrate how they used Molson Canadian's product, beer. The winner's university would be declared the number-one party school in Canada and the winner would win a trip for himself and four other friends to Cancún for spring break 2008. The contest promoted this theme: "Show everyone how you and your crew get the party started!"

For students, this sounded like a great contest: Just take dozens of entertaining photos at a party and turn them in. Better yet, grab all those pics you plan to post on Facebook anyway, submit them to the contest, and possibly win a fun-filled trip to Mexico.

However, it does not take a rocket scientist to understand why this contest was pulled before the prizes were handed out. This campaign was said to promote irresponsible drinking and offended many schools and parents. *The Globe and Mail* also commented on how encouraging students to post personal photos in drinking environments could harm their job prospects since many employers now do check up on employees and potential employees online. In fact, an article on Yahoo.com revealed that 30 percent of hiring managers use Facebook searches to research information about new and potential hires, something Molson didn't take into account when planning its campaign. Also, let's face it, the best photos are going to be those that have questionable alcohol use involved.

In trying to create brand awareness, the company overlooked the line between responsible and irresponsible behavior. Engaging students in guided dialogue might have been a better option.

On the other hand, Molson has been very successful on the

social media front with its community blog, which is consistently updated with excellent stories and photos about how Molson contributes time, resources, and money to many causes across Canada. On the "How this blog brews" pages of the site, they have a smart overview of how to participate in the community conversation, including this mission statement:

> Molson Blog aims to brew honest, friendly and courteous conversation. Please be respectful and civil to bloggers and others members of the community, even if you disagree with them.

This blog, among other recent social media initiatives, shows some great innovation from a company that is more than two hundred years old. Through this community, they also promote many face-to-face events for new friends, such as Brew 2.0, which encourages attendees to learn more about all different kinds of beer.

SONY'S PSP FLOG

The Sony flog (fake blog) "All I want for Xmas is a PSP" is perhaps one of the most famous social media campaign blunders. Numerous people outed Sony's PSP blog, figuring out that it wasn't legit. The blog was supposedly written by Charlie, a boy who was trying to persuade his friend Jeremy's parents to buy

Jeremy a PSP for Christmas. The creators even featured Charlie's supposed cousin Pete in YouTube videos associated with the blog.

The poorly disguised marketing effort was quickly squashed by those who recognized the domain name being registered to the Zipatoni ad agency. Yes, geeks online are smarter than you think—it does not take a lot of effort to look up who owns a domain name, and when dealing with an early adopter audience, such as PSP fans, you need to maintain transparency on all levels of marketing. Here is just a small sample of the hundreds of negative comments from angry consumers:

If you want a PSP badly enough you should get together with an ad agency. Then try to sell the product through a lame website while attempting to speak down to what you consider your target audience.

Comment By Jim At 12/11/2006 3:35 PM

This is bad. I really don't expect something like this from the SONY. They have there PSP game console on top yet they do this blunder. i dont understand it.

Comment By john At 12/11/2006 3:39 PM

I doubt this message will reach whoever it needs to, but Sony desperately needs to stop hiring these bozos to do their marketing. This website is as bad as the PS 3 baby ads, which are as bad as the PSP dust ball ads, which are worse than the most annoying Old Navy ad you could possibly think of.

Comment By D-stab At 12/11/2006 1:59 PM

What's even worse than launching the flog in the first place is that after Sony had been rightly accused of trying to pull off the fake site, "Charlie," the supposed blogger, continued to deny the truth in his hip youth lingo—complete with intentional spelling errors and trendy slang, including a kind of unbelievable post like this one:

we started clowning with sum not-so-subtle hints to j's parents that a psp would be teh perfect gift. we created this site to spread the luv to those like j who want a psp! consider us your own personal psp hype machine, here to help you wage a holiday assault on ur parents, girl, granny, boss— whoever—so they know what you really want.

However, it quickly become impossible for Sony to ignore the online anger any longer and it had to own up to what it did, perhaps the only smart move it made with this campaign. The company declared that it would, from now on, use the site to share real facts on the cool products the business is known for.

This is what Sony should have done from the get-go: provide information, encourage dialogue, and engage in a real-life inter-action between consumer and brand (after all, there is an army of diehard PSP fans who would have loved to participate in any-thing Sony). Do a quick search to find out more about this flog fiasco and you'll find headlines like this one from video gam-ing site Kotaku.com: "All Sony Wants for Christmas Is a Better Marketing Company." This campaign broke the first rule of Internet friending: it lacked authenticity.

RESIDENT EVIL'S VIRAL MARKETING CAMPAIGN

In 2004, Sony, the company behind the zombie survivalist video game Resident Evil: Outbreak, designed a promotional campaign through their Web site that sent out unsolicited SMS messages to mobile phones with notes like this: "I'm infecting you with t-virus." These messages would then proceed to tell the recipient to forward the message to a specific code for a chance to win prizes on a certain Web site. Though the messages did not in fact infect a person's cell phone, Sony's marketing ploy pro-voked panic when mobile phone users became worried that they had contracted a mobile phone virus (which was a pretty natural concern considering the controversial message). Cell phone company support desks were swamped with calls from message recipients who were worried that their phones were going to be harmed.

The agency that created the campaign, CE Europe, eventually sent out a press release admitting the mistake: "We had to come clean about the T-VIRUS eventually," commented Ben Le Rougetel, senior PR manager and chief virologist, CE Europe. "The T-VIRUS was originally designed to promote the release of Resident Evil: Outbreak for PS2, but it's spread much quicker than we originally anticipated. It's now totally out of control and we're not totally sure how to stop it."

This failed attempt at a viral promotional campaign was ill conceived, considering that mobile phone users would be worried about any such infection notices. Although the gaming industry does need to launch innovative marketing campaigns to be heard amid all the entertainment noise, causing panic among its target demographic is never a smart way to get a reaction.

TARGET ROUNDERS FACEBOOK CAMPAIGN

In the fall of 2007, Target, which is usually a darling of the social media marketing world, made a pretty big mistake. Its launchpad, Target Rounders, was a site where members, mostly college students, got product discounts, CDs, and other prizes for providing Target with valuable consumer feedback. Target sent out a newsletter that asked its Rounders members to join Target's Facebook group and promote it to all their friends. But here's the catch, or the big bad bold move: Target asked members to keep their involvement with the Rounders group a secret. Here's a portion of the newsletter:

> Your Mission: Try not to let on in the Facebook group that you are a Rounder. We love your enthusiasm for the Rounders, and I know it can be hard not to want to sing it from the mountaintops [and in the shower, and on the bus]. However, we want to get other members of the Facebook group excited about Target, too! And we don't want the Rounders program to steal the show from the real star here: Target and Target's rockin' Facebook group. So keep it like a secret!

In essence, Target asked members to lie.

When one member voiced her concern over this inside the Target Facebook group, she alleged that the message was quickly and suspiciously deleted. Target claimed the issue was a misunderstanding, but many members failed to see how that was the case. News about Target's "little secret" quickly spread online. Most students wanted nothing to do with trying to mislead their friends. Instead, they outed the giant retailer, believing that authenticity was more important than anything, especially among their own personal networks.

Just because a business is promoting its offerings online does not mean that proper etiquette, or "netiquette," goes out the window. The rules for good manners apply online just as they would in face-to-face conversations. Online consumers are also offline consumers and deserve the same amount of respect and transparency as any other marketing campaign is expected to deliver. Something that many companies don't understand is that the online consumer often has many more platforms to express his or her unhappiness with a business, thanks to hundreds of social media Web sites. Also, increasing a business's fan base should always be an authentic venture, especially when using social media in your marketing strategy. With a following based on trust, you can communicate more easily with your customers and eventually turn them into real friends of your brand.

Chapter eight

The Successes

As I mentioned in the introduction to this book, Tony Hsieh, CEO of Internet shoe e-tailer Zappos, is often referred to as the poster boy for doing social media right. Aside from online buzz about paying potential employees to quit before they officially start, his company has dominated the Web space with hundreds of stories of happy customers, but one particular story has always stuck in my mind. In a world where we often go online to complain about the lack of customer service we experience on a regular basis, Zappos is the exception.

"I Heart Zappos" is a blog post title from July 2007. The author, Zaz Lamarr, had ordered several pairs of shoes from Zappos for her mom, who was finding that her old shoes weren't fitting due to serious weight loss. Only two pairs fit, but Zaz was far too busy dealing with her mother's illness to return the other pairs. Soon after, her mom died. During this difficult time, Zappos had written an e-mail to Zaz asking her about the shoes. She wrote back that, because of her mother's death, she hadn't had time to return them. Going against corporate policy, Zappos arranged for UPS to pick up the shoes. Also, the shoe e-tailer sent Zaz a flower arrangement of while lilies, roses, and carnations.

Stories like this don't happen every day, but at Zappos they happen a lot more than at other companies. Tony and his team are also aware that this above-standard customer service has a huge impact on a company's success. Zaz received a couple hundred comments on her blog, including this one from user Diva:

I'd ordered shoes for myself from them before and always been happy with what I got, and never had to return them. But you can bet they'll be my first choice for shoes from now on.

Saskia wrote:

That's really something special! It's good to know there are such kind hearts in commerce.

Akrob wrote:

What a touching story! We love Zappos and that just reinforces our reason to buy our shoes from there. The customer service has always been really professional and timely. I heart Zappos as well after reading this story.

Tony, as influential as he is, is just one of many leaders who are discovering the power of social media, following the rules, and growing their business one new friend at a time. Many others are embracing this new way of marketing online. Whether you're in the business of selling footwear or promoting hardware, there is no shortage of social media case studies available online. Throughout this chapter, I've included just a small sampling of how a diverse range of companies are succeeding in the Web space. For most of them, there is not a huge up-front investment but instead some simple strategies, a few brave ideas, and a lot of listening going on.

THREADLESS "BRAND LOVE"

Threadless is an extremely popular and respected online community of designers, producers, and consumers of fun, comfy, and innovative T-shirts. Yes, these trendy tees definitely possess the cool factor, but it's the company's unique strategy that leads to its customers' loyalty. Like all successful brands in the social media space, the company believes in listening first. With their ears to the ground, or in this case the screen, Threadless lets its customers decide what the company should make.

Here's how Threadless works: The T-shirts they produce are first voted upon by the customers themselves. Threadless works through the social media channels that are most suitable to their goals, such as Facebook and Twitter, to engage with these customers.

Bob Nanna, who manages promotions, explained the company's approach to me in an e-mail: "We've learned that leveraging Facebook & Twitter has been enormous for us—especially as a company that loves to interact with our users and is also super reliant on our users," he says. "We keep our messages lighthearted and try to stay away from straight up marketing—and have interactive contests/challenges often."

For example, every week, the company's Facebook page hosts a contest where one member of the Facebook group is selected at random to get a turn at spinning a wheel to earn prizes. Customer service agents also reply to consumer complaints of dissatisfaction in a public forum online. This type of transparency and honesty is what people like to see. This openness also leads to an authentic product. Unlike some organizations that participate in social media on a semiregular basis, Threadless engages consistently with the community online. And this community is not small.

Currently, there are more than 800,000 people signed up on the Threadless site and on mailing lists, and the company is selling more than 100,000 T-shirts every month. Threadless's democratic point of view as a brand, consistent engagement with customers, and its sense of community are what make this social media strategy a huge success.

Of course, as Nanna reveals, you need to be ready for whatever traffic might come your way. Sometimes a successful social media campaign can be too successful for the infrastructure of your site. "We recently had a $9 sale on 9/9/09 that started at midnight, built up and announced on Twitter," Nanna said. "The response was so huge and immediate, it actually broke our Web site for a few hours." Who knew people would get so passionate about T-shirts? Broken Web sites due to traffic demand are a problem that most companies hope they might have with any social media work, and are definitely a sign of success.

Threadless has also been so successful with their community-building efforts that they now sell designs on their own branded T-shirts, instead of using another manufacturer. If you think this decision came from a roomful of executives, think again. The Threadless community had been asking for years that the company print on their own tees (they even got feedback from the community on the initial design). In the launch note to their audience, Threadless signed off their blog post "Love, Your friends at Threadless.com." This is a new breed of organization that considers friending and listening as part of its core.

NISSAN'S HYPERCUBE PROMO CAMPAIGN

Nissan's Hypercube social media marketing contest reached out to five hundred artistic Canadians, narrowed down from seven thousand eager volunteers, who creatively generated their own publicity and "personified the Cube brand" in an attempt to win a Nissan car. Potential winners were given the opportunity to showcase their talents at various nightclub festivities in Vancouver, Toronto, and Montreal. These Web-savvy contestants served as brand ambassadors. For example, one of the winners made a cardboard cube and drove it around Toronto. Others leveraged their online communities on sites such as Twitter to win fans. The final fifty winners were selected by online voters.

When announcing the winners, Nissan Canada's VP of sales effervesced about the success of the campaign, saying, "Hypercube is exceptional for Nissan because we are engaging with our consumers in such a relevant, unique and interactive way. The 500 finalists created an extensive online community that interacted with each other, and their local communities, and really spread the word about the Nissan Cube."

My friend Rannie Turingan, a photo blogger, won one of the cars. He was a perfect fit for the contest. His site, photojunkie.ca, is one of the most popular photo sites in Toronto. Not only did he ask his large online community to vote for him as a Cube winner, he also took some spectacular photos inside and outside the trendy car. However, it was his panoramic images from around the city of Toronto that pushed him as a finalist. Every day for a month he took spectacular pictures from different corners of the city, some of which were recommended by fans. All of this led to his big win.

What Nissan did right during this campaign was to reach out to its target demographic and participate in the places where these people were already playing online. The dancers, bloggers, actors, musicians, DJs, and others were happy to get their fifteen minutes of fame, or fifteen frames of fame, as they tried to win the hearts of fans across the country to get a free set of wheels. Nissan's contest not only excited an online audience, it also received a lot of mainstream media attention when the company handed over fifty Cubes to the happy winners who in turn shared their joy about their new rides on the Web.

DELL SOCIAL MEDIA STRATEGY

Despite previously shying away from the inevitable social media revolution, Dell is now undertaking a cross-platform strategy to create a community and engage with consumers. Dell made a significant investment in its effort to embrace the world of Web 2.0, and it's paying off to the tune of a $1 million ROI. Currently, Dell is running multiple Twitter accounts, a very active Facebook page, and a series of blogs. The blog that serves its purpose the best is "Direct 2 Dell"—home to an online content sharing community of Dell employees and consumers. Dell has also launched a project called Idea Storm—an online suggestion box—where consumers are able to share their thoughts to help Dell improve its business.

Dell's social media efforts have proven successful and are largely due to the company's extending a hand to consumers so that conversation can begin. Dell's choice to recognize and address consumer complaints publicly online has garnered it extra respect. Again, this is a perfect example of how providing the tools to engage and then listening to the conversations that result are part of a successful social media strategy.

"MY STARBUCKS IDEA" CAMPAIGN

Every time I walk out of a Starbucks store with a fancy coffee drink, I inevitably spill some on myself. It seems that the hot liquid loves to spurt up through the tiny little hole in the plastic sippy-cup lid. Fortunately, in some stores there is an alternative to Starbucks-inspired dry cleaning, thanks to a smart site.

Starbucks runs a Web property called MyStarbucksIdea.com (or MSI for short), which is an effort to embrace social media outside of the typical 2.0 diet of Facebook, Twitter, and You-Tube. Starbucks created the site, which quite simply allows consumers to share their opinions, suggestions, and ideas in a communal space where their java-lovin' voices will be heard. Furthermore, the site highlights some of the most popular suggestions and ideas, and reviews them on a regular basis. In addition to this, a blog, "Ideas in Action," was created in conjunction with the site that keeps users up-to-date on the progression of changes being made at the suggestion of those who participate (this demonstrates a thorough social media strategy, one that includes follow-up and consistency).

From flavored foam to a free drink on your birthday, the ideas are aplenty. However, it's the Splash Stick that has made the biggest buzz online. This is a thin reusable plastic stick with a stopper on top that forces your coffee to stay where it belongs, in the cup below. Now when you're walking or driving around with a Starbucks drink, you don't have to worry about spillage. This brand-new idea was thanks to the company's open suggestions online.

The Web site was created with the intent to help Starbucks get a better grasp on customer feedback and engage in extended conversations with consumers, and it has succeeded.

By listening to and leveraging the voice of the consumer, Starbucks is able to give the people improved service and products, thanks to the company's open Web forums. On its blog, the company reported that it received nearly 75,000 ideas in just six months, a pretty impressive stat. Thanks to the coffee retailer's consistency with its many online friends, MSI continues to be a popular destination for its fans.

TARGET'S "BULLSEYE GIVES" CAMPAIGN

Target is known for its smart social media campaigns—putting Walmart's copycat attempts to shame—but this one really takes the cake. The retail chain has always donated 5 percent of its income to charity, which averages out to around $3 million every week. But for a few weeks, as part of a social media charity campaign, Target created a voting application where Facebook users could vote on ten charities posted to the page. Target would then, based on the percentage of votes, donate funds to the charities. For example, if 10 percent voted for the Salvation Army, that organization would receive 10 percent of the total donations.

The simple integration with Facebook is what makes this campaign successful. By voting, users had the opportunity to post their vote on their Facebook status, which then appeared in their news feed. This type of crowd sourcing created a viral upside for the retailer because the voters' friends would see it, then perhaps they would vote and then their friends would see it. This domino effect proved to be a winner for the company, driving viewers to its Facebook page.

#BLAMEDREWSCANCER TWITTER CAMPAIGN

In May of 2009, Drew Olanoff, an avid Twitter user, was diagnosed with cancer—Hodgkin's lymphoma to be exact. In an effort to remain in good spirits, Olanoff began blaming everything from losing his keys to being stuck in traffic on his cancer. He asked everyone he knew to do the same. It caught on, and Olanoff decided perhaps he could use the running joke to make something good come out of a bad situation. Drew asked Twitter users to blame his cancer for their problems using the hashtag "#blamedrewscancer." His message quickly spread. In partnership with the Livestrong Foundation, Olanoff is now securing a deal where one dollar will be matched for every unique Twitter user who uses the hashtag. Olanoff is glad to have brought cancer to the forefront on Twitter, and also used the publicity he received to spread the word that Lance Armstrong's Livestrong Foundation isn't just intended to aid athletes and cyclists. That misconception is "Not true at all," he told me, "and I was living proof. That opened a lot of eyes in social media and changed the perception of the foundation."

In just over a month, 8,919 people have blamed Drew's cancer for 16,199 things. Lance Armstrong, Livestrong's founder, blamed Drew's cancer for a broken collarbone. Alyssa Milano blamed Drew's cancer for making her indulge in chocolate-covered popcorn. By "beating up on his cancer," Olanoff hopes to beat cancer and raise awareness.

"I've learned that the tools that we use for fun and games can be used for a more serious matter," Olanoff told me. "Good things for good causes sustain: On Twitter, for example, 'hashtag memes' usually come and go within hours. It was obvious as soon as we launched #BlameDrewsCancer that it was going to stick. It was constant, and simple enough for people to get. They also understood that not only were they blaming my cancer for something for fun, but they were raising cancer awareness with their Twitter followers, raising eyebrows and questions . . . and also potentially counting towards money going to charity. It was a perfect storm that everyone 'got' immediately."

Drew's creativity and access to a computer with Internet allowed him to create a successful charity drive and social media campaign out of virtually nothing. BlameDrewsCancer is a wonderful example of how you don't need much to achieve big results.

This initiative didn't stop after just a few weeks. For months, #blamedrewscancer continued to make an impact online. Olanoff went one step further and offered up his very catchy (and desirable) four-letter Twitter user name @drew for auction, giving all the money to cancer research. Funny guy Drew Carey answered the offer, offering one million dollars for the name (which will go to the Livestrong Foundation) if the comedian got one million followers on Twitter by December 31, 2009. To say this story has spiraled out of control, in a good way, is an understatement.

OBAMA'S SOCIAL MEDIA CAMPAIGN

Perhaps the biggest social media campaign success story of its kind is that of the grassroots movement that propelled the tech-savvy and charismatic Barack Obama into the presidency. The world's first "digital president" utilized collaborative social media tools and strategies to run a campaign that valued people first, not dollars (they came later).

This victory is due to the ingenious strategy of equipping voters with all the tools necessary to canvass—be it simply talking with friends or going door-to-door—for Obama's platform points, his vision, and so on. The networking site MyBarack-Obama provided videos, Word documents on Scribd, the ability to donate online, and countless other Web 2.0 tools, but most important, channels of discussion between Obama and voters and between voters and voters. Obama's campaign connected a country of people in an effort to bring about change for those very people, and they responded in droves.

However, as campaign volunteer and author Rahaf Harfoush said to CBC News, it's not about the technology that made Obama's digital journey to the White House a success. Rather, "It was about the fact that the campaign gave new media the opportunity to become an integrated part of the communications campaign of a political campaign."

The social media participation didn't stop when Obama became president. In fact, it continues to this day, complete with a new media director who is managing how the White House participates in the online space. Some of these initiatives have included YouTube presidential addresses, à la fireside chats. These videos routinely get more than a million views online, engaging an audience of government friends and fans (or for Obama critics, allowing them an open forum to voice their comments).

COMPARETHEMARKET.COM'S COMPARETHEMEERKAT.COM CAMPAIGN

It's easier to make T-shirts, shoes, and President Obama sexy using social media than it is to build online engagement about insurance. However, British auto insurance financial comparison site Comparethemarket.com's "Compare the Meerkat" campaign is a solid example of how a business can generate an increase in Web traffic, a rise in sales, and further brand recognition through a thoughtful combo of online and offline marketing (merging online and offline initiatives isn't always easy, but this campaign did so with great success).

The original TV ad features a charming meerkat, Aleksandr Orlov (a furry rodentlike character), expressing his frustration about how visitors are not heading to the right site for information about car insurance. And while the campaign was clever, memorable, and cute, it is the company's social media presence that continues to build an army of people who have become diehard Orlov fans.

The YouTube ad has more than 200,000 views, and hundreds of comments about the "cute" meerkat character. The video features Orlov talking about how many people are heading to ComparetheMeerkat.com (a dating site for meerkats) looking for auto insurance info when they should be going to Compare themarket.com for an easy way to save on car insurance. When you visit ComparetheMeerkat.com you get Orlov speaking to you about how you've arrived at the wrong destination and should be heading over to the car insurance site.

An Aleksandr Orlov Facebook page has hundreds of thousands of friends (aka fans) who regularly chat on Orlov's wall, waiting anxiously for a witty response from the mascot. Orlov (@Aleksandr_Orlov) has more than twenty thousand Twitter followers who read his over eight hundred tweets (not bad numbers for a company mascot!). Perhaps most amusing was an Orlov TwitPic (a photo posted to Twitter) that featured him front-and-center in an elevator with celebrity Stephen Fry (after Fry famously tweeted a picture and comment about being stuck in an elevator with a group of fellow passengers). The list of creative content generated from this campaign goes on, and like the Photoshopped TwitPic, not just from the marketing agency. Here's an example of a tweet from Orlov: "I am not really what you call 'pet' material." With this campaign, you never know what's going to come out of this character's mouth.

This campaign proves that offline marketing can serve as a catalyst for some pretty interactive and engaging online participation. Comparethemarket.com's consistency in its efforts to keep Orlov's spirit alive and kicking online keeps its dedicated community growing.

As Mashable.com reported in April 2009, this campaign was a huge social media success. Within just a few days, over three quarters of the company's monthly quotes targets were reached and over 50 percent of the site traffic in the first week was going directly to Comparethemarket.com. Most important, the number of quotes is up by 90 percent over the same period during the previous year.

When I first learned about this creative campaign, I couldn't help but add Orlov as a Twitter and Facebook friend. Sometimes I don't even understand what he's saying, but like his 600,000 fans I keep coming back for more comments like this one:

> @Aleksandr_Orlov Tomorrow is beginnings of Russia Fashion week. My invitation for be model on the MeerKatwalk have yet to arrive. I'm sure it be here soon.

Or this one:

> @Aleksandr_Orlov I have spend all weekend relaxing in Jacuzzi and now have wrinkly paws.

Following his every move online has left me rather speechless, in that I can't even believe the creativity behind this initiative. On the bravery front, it definitely gets an A+. Not many companies could pull this off. Moreover, not many people in the insurance biz have ever used social media in such a popular, rewarding, and successful way.

Chapter nine

The Future

@feather @ambermac I'm sitting right in front of you in the lounge. You interviewed me once for your show. #feelingkindofcreepy

This is a Twitter message I received while waiting to board my plane on a recent business trip. With hundreds of people staring at their laptops in the lounge, you can only imagine how difficult it was to try to find @feather in the crowd. While I peered past heads, I got another message from a friend I know.

@feather meet @ambermac. @ambermac meet @feather. You're both friends of mine—you really should know each other. :) #twitterintro

At this point I was feeling more optimistic about this @feather character, thanks to an instant digital referral from a mutual friend. After a few more back-and-forths with @feather, he finally turned around and introduced himself. Funny enough, he was actually sitting directly in front of me the entire time.

I like to tell this story because it reveals a new way of connecting online. After @feather and I started chatting, we realized how much we had in common on the business front and agreed to stay in touch. Before the prevalence of social media, chances are that we would not have talked that day. There would have been no opportunity for a face-to-face introduction. You can argue about what this says about humanity, believing that technology has made us antisocial, but I would argue back that it says that we are now able to more easily establish connections with people who are in our extended networks, even if we don't know it at first.

This in-lounge experience reminds me of Susan, the keynote attendee I mentioned at the beginning of this book. Remember her? She asked me how the Internet is changing the definition of a friend, and how this affects her business. As you have learned throughout this book, with so many new ways of building relationships online, companies are now put in a position where how well they power friend is a key to success, and to their reputation on the Web. Call this Web 3.0, or whatever you like, but the reality is that we are just at the beginning of this exciting new world. Ten years ago nobody would have been able to predict that Flickr, Facebook, or YouTube would be such big players online. Still, we all continue to wonder, what does the future hold? While I don't believe that anyone can accurately predict the advancement of technology, I do believe that we're starting to see some trends that are bound to evolve into much more. Here are a few tools to put on your social media radar as you develop your long-term strategic plans.

REAL-TIME WEB

With Web real-time search sites like Collecta and OneRiot, and the integration of Twitter and Facebook into both Google and Bing search results, the real-time Web is here, and with that comes the ability to deliver instant feedback (live updates) about a company's customer service. Listening to this stream can provide you with free, valuable data. In 2009 we saw news stories dominate the real-time Web, with stories such as Iran's presidential election and the Miracle on the Hudson topping the list. In 2010 and beyond, real-time reviews will also start to gain popularity (for example, imagine sitting in a restaurant and sharing your opinion of the food live online). The days of focus groups are just about over; now you can tap the pulse of your brand's reputation online in an instant and watch it change just as fast. This is critical when evaluating a new product launch or looking for inconsistencies in a supply chain. For advertisers, it represents a fundamental shift in serving the right ads at the right time without being intrusive.

LOCATION-BASED SERVICES

While Twitter was the social media darling of 2009, location-based services are going to be the hot topic (and valuable marketing tool) for 2010 and beyond. These services, such as Foursquare and Gowalla, allow users to check in at a certain location (via a GPS locator), notifying their friends about where they are. Each of these two services also incorporates a social gaming element, which gives users recognition for frequenting a venue a number of times. For example, on Foursquare you compete for mayorship at your favorite destinations. For businesses, this opens up a plethora of possibilities. As companies are notified about the activities of their most loyal customers, they are in turn offering coupons and incentives.

SOCIAL SHOPPING

Most people wouldn't ever consider sharing credit card statements, until social media made it a hot new trend. Blippy is changing the face of private purchasing. Just like Twitter asks the question, "What's happening?" Blippy asks "What are your friends buying?" The service lets you take all the data tied to a transaction, such as the purchase place and the amount, and sometimes the item, on your credit card statement, iTunes account, or Amazon account, and share this information with your social circle online. Like Twitter, you also follow people to get access to their updates (in this case, purchases). For example, the only shopping account I list on Blippy is my iTunes account, which reports every time I buy a song, download an app, or rent a movie. While my first reaction was to discount this service, thinking it was one social media tool that goes too far, when you play around with Blippy for a few days you realize how what your friends are buying is relevant as you want recommendations for your purchasing decisions.

QR CODES

While North America is behind other parts of the world when it comes to adopting QR technology, as I mentioned earlier in the book, this code scanning technology is ramping up here. Google's new Android phone currently has bar code scanning capability built in, and there are several apps available for the iPhone to scan QR codes.

If you are a brand builder, the world is now literally at your fingertips with advancements in mobile technology (now that the world's desktop shackles have been unlocked). Creating conversations on the go with your customers provides you an opportunity to help establish trusting (and always on) relationships and build that bridge from the world of bytes and bits to our brick-and-mortar reality.

QR codes are in the process of being included in North America by many manufacturers. Elsewhere, some big names, such as McDonald's, are already jumping on board in Japan and Korea. GE has employed a QR to launch an interactive augmented reality demonstration on your computer screen. When the user prints out a specific code and holds the paper up to their Web cam, a virtual power plant, complete with birds and a movable sun, emerges from the page (this you have to physically see to believe).

AUGMENTED REALITY (AR)

In almost every science fiction movie there are displays that overlay graphics or holograms onto the real world in order to display more information. Like the Terminator or *Star Trek's* Lt. Cmdr. Geordi La Forge's visor, computer data, combined with the real world, changes the way we behave or interact. Robocop could scan people for concealed weapons and size up potential threats. Today, that technology is no longer just a sci-fi dream, but is being used in much more powerful and creative ways in the marketing world.

While not quite virtual reality, this new technology "augments" what you see in the real world. The potential for this real-life data immersion is truly remarkable. Imagine an interactive storefront that lets passersby view a video ad, download the latest coupons and user reviews, and even ask a virtual sales assistant if that jacket in the window is available in their size at that location. However, the current iteration of this immersive technology is still cumbersome and expensive, relegated to university campuses and the R&D departments of a few high-tech firms. It requires a lot of computing power and a large and heavy backpack computer. But some companies are trying out smaller-scale versions of the technology. Best Buy has distributed an augmented reality flyer and built a Best Buy in 3D Web site that allows customers to interact with products in 3D. The popular iPhone app Urbanspoon, which uses your phone's GPS to show you what restaurants are near you, has released an update that includes AR functionality. If you point your phone's camera down the street, you get a view of the street with colored bubbles appearing over the image. Within each bubble is a rating of the restaurant, determined by how many app users "liked" the establishment or not. The bubbles vary in size depending on how far away you are from each location—the larger the bubble the closer the restaurant. As you move, the information changes to reflect where you are going.

One of the most innovative uses of AR I've seen so far came from a student in Germany, Jonas Jäger at augmentedbusiness-card.net. Jäger made a business card with AR additions that revealed his Twitter status, his portfolio, his phone number, and a hologram of him talking on his cell phone. The card leaves quite an impression. BMW, Doritos, and Wrigley's have also experimented with augmented reality advertising.

MOBILE MEET-UPS

Nowhere is this merging of the online and real worlds more evident than in the frequency and popularity of mobile-integrated events, ranging from press conferences where audience members can text or tweet questions onto a large screen where everyone can see them to social events organized and designed to bring in audiences that can't physically be there.

Twestival Global had people in 202 cities around the world connecting and raising $250,000 for a good cause: clean and safe drinking water. This was inspired and organized through Twitter by Amanda Rose, @amanda, who sent out the first tweet about the event on January 8, 2009. A thousand volunteers were recruited through Twitter and over ten thousand people participated in the global event. This caught the attention of international media outlets and brought the world together in less than 140 characters at a time. In 2010, Twestival Global is focusing on another important cause: educating the world's children. Not only does the Twestival example show the power of social networking, it also demonstrates that social media can be effective on an international scale (which cannot be said for most types of media).

In the future, companies must think seriously about the

mobile world as an integral part of the friending experience. Companies like Zappos won't just be connecting with customers via their Web site. These smart companies will be brand-building and power friending in the mobile world.

INTERNET CONNECTED DEVICES

The explosion of video game consoles, the new Kindle and other e-book readers, smart appliances, cars, GPS, and home entertainment systems are just a few devices that are linked to the Internet. This list is likely to grow as the world moves online. A Pew Internet & American Life Project survey released in the fall of 2009 found that one in five Americans now use the Internet for some sort of status update via a social network to keep up-to-date with the details of their friends' lives. The interesting takeaway from this survey was that the more devices the person used that were connected to the Internet the more likely they would be to use a status-updating service such as Twitter or Facebook. As more devices come online, more people come online. As more people come online, the mobile phone continues to take on an even more important role in developed and developing countries. To summarize Morgan Stanley analyst Mary Meeker's presentation at the 2009 Web 2.0 Summit in San Francisco, the mobile Web is taking over the world with next-generation platforms (such as social networking) driving unprecedented change in communications and commerce. Simply put . . . look out world. We have a mobile revolution in our hands.

OPEN SOCIAL NETWORKS

People often complain of log-in fatigue. Having so many user passwords to remember limits the number of social networks people want to join. As much value as they may get out of some of them, they just don't feel like signing up and filling out biographical fields one more time. So they move on. As I mentioned at the beginning of this book, I am a member of many social networks, including Facebook, Twitter, LinkedIn, MySpace, Ning, Blippy, and many others. I spend most of my time on Facebook and Twitter because, quite frankly, I can't be bothered with the hassle of logging in to my other accounts on a regular basis. In the future, this experience will be much different and it will affect how companies use social networking to build brands.

Think about it like this. When e-mail first came out, many of us simply had one e-mail account. If we had two accounts, we were required to log into two separate interfaces. With the introduction of services such as Gmail and Yahoo Mail, we can now have as many e-mail accounts as we want coming into one stream—whether it's for work or for personal use.

The same thing will happen for social networks. Individuals will belong to more social networks because the system for accessing these social networks will be seamless, whether you belong to one or ten. This will open up a unique opportunity for companies using social networking to build online relationships. Instead of worrying about asking its customers to join yet another social network, as a company such as Starbucks might do right now with its online community, companies will soon be able to take advantage of having no more walled gardens. This means that companies need to start thinking about creating customized social networks to start the relationship-building process today.

Organizations like DiSo and others are trying to build and integrate open-source, meaning nonproprietary, codes in the building of everything on the Web. In the spring of 2009 Facebook announced that it had joined Open ID, which led to wide media commentary that this would be the first step to open networks.

PEOPLE-POWERED CUSTOMER SERVICE

John O'Day had a beef with Whole Foods in Cupertino, California. He believed that the high-end grocery store was possibly spraying tuna with chemicals to keep the color bright, suggesting that it was a cost-cutting measure for the store, even though Whole Foods was supposed to offer healthy products. Instead of talking to the store manager, John went to getsatisfaction.com, a new Web site that hosts conversations between companies and their customers.

John's complaint did not go unnoticed. Slaton Carter, a Whole Foods Market team member, quickly answered John's complaint on the Get Satisfaction site, letting the customer know that their "fish must meet stringent quality standards, one of which is that a product cannot contain artificial preservatives, colors, flavors, and sweeteners." Slaton then commented that if John's question was not answered, he would do his best to get him a more thorough reply. Soon after, John thanked Slaton for taking an interest in his comment and thanked him again for addressing his complaint directly.

Within a few sentences, Whole Foods turned an unhappy customer into a happy customer. John's story is just one of thousands on Get Satisfaction, an online forum for companies to engage in conversations with customers. Companies using the customer service site include Adobe, the BBC, Dell, and more than ten thousand others. Get Satisfaction is a free service for the public, and a paid service for companies. Each company ensures that it has employees checking conversations related to its products, saving time and money in terms of online support.

The Whole Foods story is just one example of how people-powered customer service will be an Internet friending trend in the future. The Web has routinely been a place for customers to complain, but now companies are starting to understand how important it is to be part of this conversation. Not only can engaging a customer win you a customer for life, building a relationship with this customer is a brand-building investment that more and more companies will value down the road.

CONCLUSION

One main reason that the tools and methods of executing social media are so complex is because they have so much to offer in return. Never before have we lived in a world where measuring traffic and interest has been so easy and exact. With such an overwhelming amount of powerful data at our fingertips, it can be tempting to just panic and revert to the old way of doing things.

However, I hope that after reading this book you are filled with the passion, knowledge, and commitment you need to build a social media strategy, starting from the inside out. Whether you're an international star, such as Tony Robbins, or a one-person team in a small rural town, nurturing online connections is critical for your business to survive, and critical to keep your business relevant in the years to come. If you follow the three rules of authenticity, bravery, and consistency, pick the right tools for the job, and learn from the successes and mistakes of others, you should be well on your way to friending in a powerful new way.

Acknowledgments

My one-year-old son Connor doesn't know it yet, but he made writing this book possible. Some people say that having a child means you can't get anything done. I would argue the opposite. Not only did his frequent naps and strict schedule provide me with quiet and focused writing time; while working on *Power Friending* I constantly thought of how the Internet is going to affect his life in so many profound ways.

Connor's dad, my fiancé, sat with me through endless nights to make sure I hit all my deadlines. (Who I am kidding, we were up with the baby anyway!) He also filled my inbox with hundreds of social media stats and stories that are the backbone of this book. Simply put, Chris is my rock.

My parents, Bev and Doug, and my brother, Jeff, also deserve a huge thank you, mostly for supporting my inner geekdom. From the cover to the contents, they provided me with feedback along the way. As for other family members, I can't forget a big shout-out to my grandmother Eve and my late grandmother Freda—these amazing women gave me the courage to do anything in life, even if they never truly understood what I do for a living. Finally, on the personal side, I want to thank our nanny, Laura, for caring for Connor when we needed her most.

On the professional side, David Lavin and his gang at my speaking bureau (The Lavin Agency) hooked me up with my book agent John Boswell and his associate Emily Winter. Thank you, thank you, thank you. If it wasn't for all of you, I would have nowhere to express my passion for the social web. Also, my editor Courtney and the fine folks at Portfolio deserve a medal for making writing this book one of the most enjoyable experiences of my life. What an amazing team.

Last, I have to thank Catherine Faas for helping me to keep my research intact and my many interviews on track. You are amazing—don't ever leave me. To my many Internet friends, I hope you enjoy *Power Friending* and know that I could never have done this without you. See you online.

Notes

Page

9. Zappos is famous for sharing its hiring and firing strategies on the web. **Source:** Adweek.com

16. Ward Christensen develops the first electronic board system (BBS). **Source:** SocialMediaRockstar.com

17. Jarkko Oikarinen creates the first Internet relay chat (IRC). **Source:** SocialMediaRockstar.com

17. World Wide Web is widely available to the public. **Source:** SocialMediaRockstar.com

17. IBM designs the first smartphone prototype. **Source:** USAToday.com

17. IBM smartphone prototype sells for approximately $900. **Source:** Byte Magazine

17. Instant messaging soars to popularity. **Source:** SocialMedia Rockstar.com

18. Napster shakes up the music world. **Source:** SocialMediaRockstar.com

18. LiveJournal helps bring blogging to the masses. **Source:** Social MediaRockstar.com

18. Friendster kicks off the online friending phenomenon. **Source:** ApolloMediaBlog.com

20. Web 2.0 is born. **Source:** O'Reilly Network

20. Facebook has 300 million users, and counting. **Source:** Facebook-Advertising-Marketing.com

20. YouTube is acquired by Google for $1.65 billion. **Source:** TechCrunch.com

21. Apple includes a podcast directory in 2005, propelling the term *podcasting* into the mainstream. **Source:** HawaiiUP.com

21. Unfriend is named the *New Oxford Dictionary*'s word of the year. **Source:** PCWorld.com

26. Number of Facebook users over fifty-five grew from 1 million to nearly 6 million during a six-month period in 2009. **Source:** InsideFacebook.com

31. Over one third of U.S. Facebook users are over age thirty-five and about half of that group is over forty-five. **Source:** ScottMonty.com

34. Bill Tancer concludes social media activities have surpassed porn online. **Source:** Reuters.com

34. Ninety-five percent of businesses say they plan to use social media. **Source:** USAToday.com

34. Eighty percent of companies use or plan to use LinkedIn to find employees. **Source:** JobVite.com

35. If Facebook were a country, it would be the world's fourth largest. **Source:** PodcastingNews.com

35. Seventy-eight percent of social media users interact with companies or brands via new media sites and tools. **Source:** Econsultancy.com

45. One hundredy ninety thousand friends had been sacrificed within a week after launching the Whopper Sacrifice Application. **Source:** ABC2News.com

47. The "MotrinGate" damage was made worse by the failure to react bravely and quickly to the backlash. **Source:** AdAge.com

50. Sophie giraffe, created in France in 1961, has sold millions and millions of their teethers. **Source:** CheekyMonkey.ca

58. Articulate E-Learning blog has more than 20,000 subscribers. **Source:** ReadWriteWeb.com

61. Southwest Airlines monitors tweets and Facebook statuses to engage with customers. **Source:** ReadWriteWeb.com

62. Tyson Foods reaches out to Twitter users and receives increased discussion around Hunger Relief. **Source:** FastCompany.com

63. Paula Drum helps H&R Block set up online community Digits. **Source:** JenniferJones.com

65. YouTube receives more daily eyeballs than the top television networks in the United States combined. **Source:** Broadcast Engineering.com

65. YouTube jumps from 30 million to 1 billion views per day. **Source:** Mashable.com

65. Thirteen hours of video uploaded to YouTube every minute. **Source:** TheFutureBuzz.com

66. Average length of a YouTube video is just under three minutes. **Source:** TheFutureBuzz.com

67. Will It Blend? campaign helps drive up sales of the consumer blender by 500 percent. **Source:** Mashable.com

68. Alltop is an online magazine rack that lets users create personalized RSS readers. **Source:** Alltop.com

71. TWiT.tv network launches in 2005. **Source:** TWiT.tv

72. *CBA PracticeLink* podcast is one of the highest in demand among Canadian lawyers and is offered in a variety of file formats. **Source:** Market2World.com

72. Whirlpool's *American Family* podcast boasts tens of thousands of listeners at only a year old. **Source:** Online.WSJ.com

75. Barnes & Noble launches bookstore iPhone app in 2009. **Source:** MobileMarketingWatch.com

76. Marvel Comics' Stan Lee releases iPhone app Jumper. **Source:** MobileMarketingWatch.com

76. ING releases free T-Mobile G1 augmented reality app. **Source:** AdverbBlog.com

61. Nike's award-winning "Shoot Your Colors" campaign is a hit. **Source:** MobiadNews.com

77. Pet Shop Boys release a video in 2007 with its own QR code. **Source:** Engadget.com

78. Kraft Foods used SMS messages to promote new brand of instant coffee. **Source:** MobileMarketer.com

78. Axe launches "Little Black Book" ring tone giveaway campaign. **Source:** Christine.net

79. Wikipedia has over 13 million user-generated articles. **Source:** Socialnomics.net

81. Nokia estimates that 20 percent of its 68,000 employees use wiki pages to update schedules, project statuses, etc. **Source:** Elearningpost.com

81. Disney's Pixar studio used a wiki to manage production on *WALL-E*. **Source:** Online.WSJ.com

82. Award-winning firm Red Ant uses a wiki as a collaboration hub for both employees and customers. **Source:** Atlassian.com and Red Ant.com.au

84. Apple dominates mobile app world. **Source:** RoughlyDrafted.com

85. Google's Android app platform is growing rapidly. **Source:** Gizmodo.com

89. One in eight couples married in the United States in 2008. **Source:** McKinsey.com

105. Eight million users become fans of Facebook pages every day. **Source:** Facebook.com

106. Each person on Facebook (worldwide) has approximately 150 friends in their network. **Source:** TheFutureBuzz.com

110. Social networking is more popular than e-mail. **Source:** Mashable .com

114. The number of people using social media grew from 17 percent of Internet users to 26 percent of Internet users. **Source:** eMarketer .com

117. More than 20,000 Best Buy employees are members of Blue Shirt Nation. **Source:** BusinessInnovationFactory.com

117. Blue Shirt Nation boosts Best Buy employee 401(K) enrollment by 30 percent. **Source:** TwinCities.BizJournals.com

119. More than 85 percent of U.S. marketing executives agreed that customer engagement is the most important benefit of social media marketing. **Source:** eMarketer.com

120. Eight-six percent of professionals across a variety of fields experiment with social media, and of that group, only sixteen percent measure ROI. **Source:** Smurdoff.com

122. Virgin Atlantic airlines releases iPhone app (for $4.99) for those afraid of flying. **Source:** Virgin-Atlantic.com

126. Mattel launches The Playground Community. **Source:** Communi Space.com

141. MySpace's traffic drops to 60 percent fewer than Facebook. **Source:** Compete.com

142. Flickr hosts more than 3.6 billion images. **Source:** TheStandard.com

142. Ning boasts over 1 million networks. **Source:** TechCrunch.com

153. YouTube is the number one video sharing site, boasts 1 billion views per day, and is the second most widely used search engine after Google. **Source:** TGDaily.com

159. Bill Wasik creates the first ever flash mob. **Source:** Journal .FiberCulture.org

160. Nielsen study suggests texting is now more popular than voice mail. **Source:** Wired.com

176. In the fall of 2006 Laura and Jim begin to document their "Wal-Marting Across America" journey, but it is revealed to be a hoax produced by Edelman PR. **Source:** BusinessWeek.com

177. Skittles launches ill-conceived Twitter campaign in March 2009. It fails and is pulled. **Source:** JoanneJacobs.net

179. GM launches Chevy Tahoe user-generated video contest at a bad time, and it fails. **Source:** MentalFloss.com

181. Walmart launches second social media campaign (Facebook "Roommate Style Match") and it fails too, while a better-planned similar campaign by Target succeeds. **Source:** Wikinomics.com

182. BringPopcorn.com launches spam campaign to reach high ranks on Digg, gets busted, and is blacklisted. **Source:** BlogHerald.com

184. Pizza Hut hires "twintern" and receives a great deal of flack. **Source:** TechCrunch.com

186. Molson Canadian launches "The Molson Canadian Nation Campus Challenge" in 2007 which ends up getting pulled due to the company indirectly promoting irresponsible drinking. **Source:** MarketingPilgrim.com

187. Thirty percent of hiring managers use Facebook searches to research information about new and potential hires. **Source:** Yahoo.com

188. Sony launches fake "All I Want for Xmas is a PSP" blog and readers quickly out the company for their dishonesty. **Source:** Consumerist.com

191. In 2007, Sony launches promotional campaign that sent out unsolicited SMS messages and it backfires when concerned recipients worry the ads are viruses due to a poor design. **Source:** The Register.co.uk

192. In 2007, Target makes the mistake of launching "Target Rounders," where they asked their members to lie. **Source:** Blog.ThoughtPick .com

197. More than 800,000 people are signed up on Threadless and the company sells more than 100,000 T-shirts every month. **Source:** News.Cnet.com

200. Nissan launches Hypercube campaign and reaches out to five hundred artistic Canadians, and hands out fifty Cubes to the happy winners. **Source:** Newswire.ca

201. Dell gets ROI of $1 million. **Source:** WebTrafficROI.com

202. Starbucks creates MyStarbucksIdea.com site to great reviews. **Source:** Mashable.com

203. MyStarbucksIdea.com received nearly 75,000 ideas in just 6 months. **Source:** Forrester.com
203. Target's "Bullseye Gives" campaign donates approximately $3 million to a charity chosen by users every week for the duration of the campaign. **Source:** TmwMedia.com
204. Drew Olanoff gets 8,919 people to blame 16,199 things on #Blame drewscancer in just over a month. **Source:** BlameDrewsCancer .com
206. Drew Carey purchases @drew for $1 million. **Source:** Mashable .com
207. ComparetheMeerkat YouTube ad gets more than 200,000 views and hundreds of comments. **Source:** BrandRepublic.com
209. ComparetheMeerkat campaign is a huge success, reaching over 50 percent of the site traffic goals in the first week after its launch. Number of quotes goes up by 90 percent. **Source:** Mashable.com
215. Google's new Android phone already has QR bar code scanning ability, and iPhones have available apps to do the same thing. **Source:** Mashable.com
216. QR technology is in the process of being included in North America by many manufacturers. **Source:** CenterNetworks.com
217. Best Buy distributes AR flyer and 3-D Web site that allows customers to interact with products in 3-D. **Source:** Gizmodo.com
218. Twestival had people in 202 cities worldwide raise over $250,000 in a single day. **Source:** Mashable.com
222. Companies like Adobe, BBC, Dell, and more than 10,000 others use the GetSatisfaction.com service. **Source:** Getsatisfaction.com

Index